W O R K B

FINDING POWER, PASSION AND JOY *BEING AT WORK*

A Unique Coaching System for Becoming Your Own Mentor and Leader

mary a. brandon • prudence a. cole • robert s. hunsberger

Traverse City, Michigan

FINDING POWER, PASSION AND JOY BEING AT WORK
A Unique Coaching System for Becoming Your Own Mentor and Leader
by Mary A. Brandon, Prudence A. Cole, Robert S. Hunsberger

Published by:

BookMarketingSolutions,LLC
The Publisher of Experts

10300 E. Leelanau Ct.
Traverse City MI 49684 U.S.A.
orders@BookMarketingSolutions.com
www.BookMarketingSolutions.com

All rights reserved. No part of this book may be reproduced or transmitted in any form or by any means, electronic or mechanical, including photocopying, recording or by any information storage and retrieval system, without written permission from the publisher, except for the inclusion of brief quotations in a review.

Copyright © 2006 by Mary A. Brandon, Prudence A. Cole, Robert S. Hunsberger

Legacy Technique Copyright © 2001-2006 by Aspect Consulting. Used by permission.

Brandon, Mary.

   Finding your power, passion and joy being at work : a unique
coaching system for becoming your own mentor and leader / Mary A.
Brandon, Prudence A. Cole, Robert S. Hunsberger. — Traverse City, MI :
Book Marketing Solutions, 2005.

        p. ; cm.

   Includes bibliographical references and index.
   ISBN: 0-9741345-2-X

  1. Job satisfaction. 2. Quality of work life. 3. Success in
business. I. Brandon, Mary. A. II. Cole, Prudence. A III. Hunsberger, Robert. S. IV. Title.

HF5549.5.J63 B73 2005
658.3/1422—dc22   0506

Project coordination by BookMarketingSolutions.com

*"In a word, each man is questioned by life;
and he can only answer to life by answering for his own life;
to life he can only respond by being responsible."*

— Viktor E. Frankl, *Man's Search For Meaning*

Dedication

We would like to dedicate our book to Mary's parents, Mary Lou Brandon and Roderick John Brandon, who passed on during the writing. Mary's parents were and still are her encouragement to do whatever she could dream and gave her a creative and tenacious inheritance. The blessing of their gifts will always be remembered.

FINDING YOUR POWER, PASSION AND JOY *BEING* AT WORK

In Acknowledgement

We have learned that writing a book is a difficult, time consuming and daunting project, which would not come to fruition without the support and help of family and friends. With gratitude and love, we would like to thank the following people for helping us complete this book.

First and foremost we thank our families: Donna Brandon for all of your hard work in laying out the initial book and for sharing the vision of this possibility and future ones, as well your brilliant mind. Traverse Brandon Jurcisin, Mary's young son, for being so patient while she spent many hours working at the computer, and for his insight and creative input in choosing our title. Sue Brandon for her help with our quotes. Dick Klimisch, Prudence's husband, for his patience and persistence in reading our initial drafts and gently guiding us to a better book. Norma Hunsberger, for her patience, encouragement, and support, believing that we could do this. Lastly, our parents, who encouraged us to do whatever we could dream and were catalysts to our individual success in so many ways.

We thank our friends: Marie Harl, Chris Pineau, Mike Flynn, Dan Snyder, Rita Daniels, Gerilyn Gruzwalski, Pat Anderson, Lori Schehr, and Diane Reed who read and worked with versions of this book to help us improve it. Tom White, our publisher and partner who believed in this book and us. Robert Williams, Larry and Ellen Miller, Tom Schehr, Buck Buchanan, Buck Bodwell, Teresa Tschirky and Mike Reed for their coaching, expertise and encouragement over the years. Karen Riggen and Tari Nikkila for making it possible for Mary to make the trip to Traverse City that would help bring this project to reality. Lorraine Weber and the EarthWalk community for all the teachings that show up in so many ways in our work because that is how deeply and profoundly you have impacted us and the work that we do.

We would also be remiss if we didn't acknowledge our histories. The US Marine Corps, which gave Bob profound leadership lessons and experiences. EDS, providing Bob and Prudence significant leadership development opportunities and experiences as well as a cadre of wonderful friends and supporters. Mary's work in Aspect Consulting Inc. through partnerships with the State of Michigan and Community Mental Health Programs. With special acknowledgement to Chuck Stockwell, James Bunton and Cecily Molyneaux for their inspiration and motivation, so instrumental to Aspect's success. And Aspect, for being the system of support that it has been for many and a realized dream for Mary, for which she is eternally grateful.

A special thanks to our customers who have supported our work with their individual successes, especially Henry Ford Health Systems and Bob Riney, the Michigan Department of Career Development, Vocational Rehabilitation Services, particularly Wayne County and Oakland County offices.

Lastly, a thank you to our dear clients, both past and present, who have coached us as we have coached them. With a special thanks to each other for being such a wonderful team to create and have fun with.

Contents

In Acknowledgement	vii
Foreword	xiii
Introduction	xv
This is Our Story	xvi
How Has Your Journey Been So Far?	xviii
Our Commitment to This Work and to You	xvii
Five Key Messages	xviii
Chapter 1: Ready To Begin	1
Where Do You Start?	1
Why Build a Portfolio?	2
How Does the Process Work?	2
How Will a Portfolio Work for You?	3
Chapter 2: What Is Your Story?	5
Where Are You?	5
Work Health Assessment	7
Your Stories	14
Life Facets	20
Life Purpose	23
Chapter 3: Know Thyself	27
Who Are You?	27
Assessment Versus Observations	28
The Whole is Greater Than The Sum of the Parts	28
The Fun and the Warning in Using Categorization!	29
Life Interests	30
Character Traits	38
Personal Style	44
Putting It All Together, *being*	53
Your Beliefs	53
Life Purpose Statement	55

Chapter 4: Success: Using Your Talents — 57
What You Bring to the Job — 57
Aptitudes and Skills — 59
Putting It All Together, *doing* — 64
Your Beliefs — 65
Life Purpose Statement — 67
Gathering — Employment History — 70

Chapter 5: The Right Fit — 75
What Will Work for You? — 75
True Values — 77
Preferred Employer — 84
Work Environment — 90
Putting It All Together, *having* — 95
Your Beliefs — 95
Life Purpose Statement — 97

Chapter 6: Getting Where You Are Going — 99
Setting Your Course — 99
Roles and Goals — 101
Finding Your Joy — 108
Life Purpose Statement — 110
Dream Work — 111

Chapter 7: Making It Happen — 115
Ready, Set, Go! — 115
Career Plan — 117
Work Template — 123

Chapter 8: Your Credentials, Please! — 129
Gathering — Training and Education — 129

Chapter 9: Highlighting Your Work — 135
Gathering — Work Examples — 135

Chapter 10: In Honor of Recognition — 139
Gathering — Awards and Honors — 139

Chapter 11: In Service to the Community — 143
Gathering — Community Service — 143

Chapter 12: For Members — 147
Gathering — Professional Memberships and Activities — 147

Chapter 13: Endorsing the Product (Yes, that's you!)   **151**
Gathering — References and Endorsements   151

Chapter 14: Is This the End?   **155**
Using Your Portfolio   155
Keep It Current
Customizing Your Portfolio

Success   **159**

Contacting Us   **160**

Appendix   **161**

Bibliography   **162**

Index   **164**

Foreword

In 21st century organizations, much attention is being given to coaching and mentoring as a tool for improving performance and developing individuals in their careers. Most of that effort is driven by the organization or employer, and too little attention is given to the personal responsibility of individuals for their own self-development.

Self-development is the ability to take an accurate look at your own strengths and development needs, including the impact that you have on others. Self-development also represents a willingness to address those needs through self-directed learning, and by trying new approaches.

For successful self-development, you must routinely seek feedback from others —- including those who are likely to be critical —- and appreciate the need to learn and grow. In reflecting on your own performance, you learn what to avoid from less successful events and reinforce the positive gained from more successful events in your life. Having done this, annual improvement goals may be set.

In understanding the impact that you have on others, you must be aware of which behaviors and styles get the best results. Then you must modify your behavior in response to informal cues as well as formal feedback. Success comes from integrating results and personal development goals.

Up until now, there has been no set of guidelines or primer for self-development that individuals can turn to as a source of guidance. *Finding Power, Passion and Joy Being at Work* responds to this need by leading the reader through a set of messages, exercises and guidelines for self-development.

It begins by establishing the reality of self-accountability through a set of five messages about work and what it has to offer the individual. That is followed by an effort to help the reader understand how to build their own portfolio of stories that relates their work to their quality of life.

The workbook helps the reader get to know their characteristics, traits, life interests, behavioral tendencies, and personal beliefs. It directs them to exercises on how to recognize their talents, learn which organizations might be a good fit, establish their credentials, get to where they want to go and achieve their life purpose and dream work.

Anyone who follows these guidelines will not only meet but exceed the requirements of self-development, be an asset to their organization and improve their quality of life. I highly recommend this book to anyone who feels they need a coach, for that coach is themselves.

> *"It's never too late to be what you might have been."*
>
> — George Elliot

Foreword by Gail L. Warden, President Emeritus, Henry Ford Health System

"A discovery is said to be an accident meeting a prepared mind."

—Albert Szent-Gyorgyi

Introduction

Welcome to our world of coaching and your opportunity to find *power, passion and joy*! This process is going to take you on an exciting journey of discovery about what you have to bring to your world of work and what work has to offer you. We will coach you to take responsibility for your work life, so you can become your own mentor and leader.

Together we bring over half a century of knowledge and experience navigating our own careers, with both opportunities and disappointments, allowing us to recognize that work can be an exciting, pleasurable and fulfilling part of life. Work can provide the opportunity to achieve great things and help you realize your **Life Purpose**; it does not have to be a painful and burdensome experience. Since, when it is all said and done, we will each spend close to 45 years of our life working, why wouldn't we want that time to be enjoyable?

We three authors are a very diverse lot. We have worked as master coaches to support individuals who want more from their work. This book comes from a desire to make our coaching accessible to everyone. We know that what was true for us is true for you, and we have the skills and talents to support you in **Finding Power, Passion and Joy Being at Work**.

This is Our Story

We like to say that while our writing partnership would appear somewhat unusual, the combination was the only way this book could occur. You will see that although we advocate planning and goal setting to accomplish your dreams, we are living testament to the purpose of a higher power, and the strength and determination of the human spirit, along with a little luck and serendipity!

Mary probably began studying people from the moment she was born. This natural curiosity led her to educate herself within the fields of psychology, philosophy and other social sciences including metaphysics. She has always loved to learn and reads voraciously, reveling in information that would enhance the human experience. Her interests have been a magnetic force in her work life, drawing her first to service oriented positions, then a career in vocational counseling, business ownership, motherhood and now to the role of author. From her experiences in vocational counseling, she became very intrigued with how and why people make their choices. She concluded that our life, and perhaps even the reason we are here, is defined by our *self*, who we *authentically are*. That *self* is the compass by which we can navigate our life. Mary believes, as a result of her research, that every person is deeply creative, rich in potential *entrepreneurial* spirit, a belief that has guided the work for her company, Apsect Consulting Inc. What she offers is support in finding and following your heart as your mentor, discovering the leadership of your natural inherent character, to not only "find," but also to *own*, Power, Passion and Joy.

Prudence's career began after college and like many, followed a profession that was more a reflection on society and women's roles than an actual direction. While **being** a teacher was rewarding work, it did not provide the challenge and opportunity she craved. It also did not provide an outlet for her management and leadership abilities. Leaving the teaching profession led to a position with the government and from there positions with steadily increasing responsibility in corporate America. Thus there was a pattern of recognizing what she needed and wanted from work, and a willingness to take the risks to achieve it. Ultimately, she reached her goal of executive leadership and then walked away from it all to pursue her dream of her own business, being@work, Inc. Now, having achieved her goal of a leadership and work life coaching company, she knows that even when it looks like you have all your dreams coming true, there is always more!

Bob has over 40 years of experience in leadership and professional development training programs. Early indicators of Bob's career were visible as a young boy: Bob loved playing soldier. It was no surprise that after high school he joined the Marine Corps, where he had a very successful military career. Once retired from the Marines, Bob took his leadership and counseling skills to corporate America, where he managed and taught others in corporate organizations about employee and leadership development. In addition, he has been a keynote and motivational speaker, and a consultant in the areas of professional and individual development. He has taught thousands of people how to better manage their occupational and personal lives. Now, retired for the second time (bringing a whole new meaning to the word) he has embarked on his third career as R.S. Hunsberger Consulting, Inc., a professional development consultant and writer. In addition he is an associate of being@work sharing his leadership and coaching skills with others. Bob's writing adventures express how individual lives can and have impacted history. This interest has made it natural for him to help others be the force of their actions, becoming their own leaders.

Whether your work history is as a businessperson, entrepreneur, member of the military, homemaker or student, you have accomplished many things that have shaped you into who you are. It is our belief that by completing this process, you will identify what opportunities are in front of you, understand the lessons you've learned, acknowledge your gifts and recognize your purpose for **being** at work.

Introduction

How Has Your Journey Been So Far?

Do you believe you can't *be, do* or *have* what you want? Do you know how to mentor yourself? Do you have fears about work? What perceptions about work have you assumed to be a reality and continue to perpetuate? Is your career a total accident, or something for which you have thoroughly prepared and planned? Are you your own leader, or are your waiting for someone to rescue you? We suspect, if you are like most people, you have grappled with these questions at some point in your life.

So how can you address them? One way is by taking responsibility for your career; easily said, and actually easily done with our help. You can start by discovering your interests, aptitudes, and abilities and skills, as well as what tends to get you stuck. You can gather your work history so that you can give meaning to the things you have done and the outcomes you have experienced. You can set goals and a direction that you are invested in, that have meaning, and that align with your purpose. In doing this, you will effect positive change in your work life that can begin immediately.

Our Commitment to This Work and to You

One way to set the process of manifestation into motion is to look at what you want to *have*, and then ask yourself what you think you would have to *be* and then *do* in order to achieve it. This is the *be, do, have* paradigm. *Being* who you are, "the state of well-*being*," naturally inspires you into actions (the *doing*). What you can *have* is the end result of what you are *being* and comfortably *doing*. Another way to understand this is that *having* is what results from *being* and then *doing*.

In our experience, many times the problem is not knowing what is truly desired. Thus, the approach that we take in our book is to have you engage in creating a "living" career portfolio. Using our process, you will be able to identify your relationship to work, as well as to others, in both your personal life and in the workplace. This process helps you pinpoint your assets. You will be able to determine what you desire and create synergy with others who can support you in your goals. You will know if you are in the right place, and decisions will tend to become easier. You will have "fit the pieces together" to create a balanced picture of yourself, positioning yourself for career opportunities that enable self-fulfillment.

Your living career portfolio will cause you to become the expert on you, so that *you* can be your own mentor and leader and make the best choices for your life. It is a process that grows with you and maintains its relevance as you continue to learn how to inspire yourself into actions that will change your life!

The world of work has definitely changed. These are times not only of multiple jobs, but multiple careers. Traditional leadership roles and forms of structure are changing. It is common to hear that there are no longer such things as loyalty or job security. Mistrust and manipulation appear to be far too commonplace. The good news is that our collective workplace has become more diverse, with many different perspectives. So being prepared for change and opportunities is not only a smart use of your time, but will enable you to make the wisest choices when the time comes to make them. You don't have to wait for a problem or crisis to motivate you, or for any outside force to move you. There is no time like the present to get started.

> ***"Your vision will become clear only when you can look into your own heart.***
> ***Who looks outside, dreams; who looks inside, awakes."***
>
> —Carl Jung

Five Key Messages

In all our years of working, we have learned that there are some truths, which when understood, begin the process of moving forward. To prepare for this work, we ask you to read through these truths and think about them. We guarantee that you will view these messages differently as you move through this process.

Message 1
"If you don't care where you are going, it doesn't matter which way you go."

In a conversation between Alice and the Cheshire Cat in the book *Alice in Wonderland*, the cat points to a well understood fact: Successful people know where they are going and what they want to achieve in life. Many have defined their life purpose. Without a purpose or direction, you just wander around, and therefore it doesn't matter which way you go. Your completed living career portfolio will be your road map to your goals and life purpose.

Message 2
"No one is coming!"

The reality is, it is up to you. No one is going to come and tell you what to do or define your life purpose. No one is going to rescue you from your current situation. Even from a spiritual perspective, if you believe that a higher power will do it for you, you still must be aware enough and able to see the opportunities that are put before you. You have to be willing to take the risks necessary to move forward. This is where fear tends to stall people from making a change. It is up to you to take action, provide your own support, and become your own mentor and leader.

Message 3
"You don't have to do anything you don't want to do, except die!"

Many individuals believe they cannot achieve their dreams because of what they feel they have to do. They believe they no longer have a choice. This becomes an excuse and a self-made trap. You always have a choice. The sooner you realize that what you have to do is really what you have chosen to do, the sooner you reclaim your power and take responsibility for your situation. This includes what you believe about having the "right stuff," such as an advanced degree, a friend in the business, or a natural born talent. I "have to" becomes no different than an excuse.

Message 4
"Life is full of trade-offs."

Each decision we make has consequences, and making a decision with an understanding of what you might gain and what you might lose is taking full responsibility for that decision. Another way we talk about this is "choosing which problem you are willing to live with." This message prompts us to think about what is really important to us and what we really need to have in our lives. Having choices means taking the responsibility for what you get and what you give up. No one can ever tell you what to *do*, although many people may try. You are the only one who will live with the end results of your decisions, and you are the only one who knows what it means to you.

Message 5
"There is no failure, only feedback."

Failure is defined as an omission of performance, or lack of success, but describing omissions or lack as failing is to miss out on the opportunity they provide. When we focus on failing, we are talking about outcomes; when we focus on feedback, we are talking about the opportunity to improve and grow. You could say Thomas Edison failed at over 2,000 experiments, or that he developed the light bulb from the feedback he received from those 2,000 experiments. Failures, or mistakes, are learning opportunities for growth, improvement and innovation. After all, if you were always right and knew just what to do, life would not be very adventurous.

Why have we included these messages? Throughout this book, you will be prompted to analyze and reflect on your work and decide whether one of the five messages could apply to your present thinking or way of *being*. Are you willing to let go of something that always has worked for you, or at least are you willing to open up a little and look at it another way? Your reaction to these messages can indicate a gap or block in how you are *being*, and therefore in what you end up *doing*, and thus, ultimately, *having*.

Enjoy your adventure, and congratulations on taking this step toward improving your life and your living!

"Everyday I get up and look through the Forbes list of the richest people in America. If I'm not there, I go to work."

— Robert Orben

Ready To Begin

This is the beginning of our process to build the work life you desire and create your Portfolio! This system is designed to provide a self-coaching structure to explore your skills, talents, experience, learning, and most importantly, your own magnificence to *"find your power, your passion and your joy."* When you have completed this work, you will know who you are and what you want. You will be ready to take action to accomplish your goals and then be able to achieve them.

Where Do You Start?

In our coaching, we begin with the **Work Health Assessment** in chapter 2. It is designed to provide an initial diagnosis of where you are and what might be keeping you stuck. (You may also choose to answer the questionnaire online at www.beingatwork.com and receive automated feedback. You have an additional option to obtain personalized feedback by going to www.marybrandon.com. From there, you will begin the task of identifying and exploring your *power, passion and joy*.

Your first assignment is an important one — writing **Your Stories**. In this defining exercise, you will write about those times of your life that impacted and molded you into who you are today. We encourage you not to skip or make light of this activity. It is a major underpinning for the exercises in this book. One way to think about these stories is that they contain the secrets about who you have **been** — your power.

Then you will explore the particulars of identifying your *passion*! Each step along the way builds on your accumulation of knowledge and insight about you. Where do you spend your time, in which **Life Facets**, and where would you like to? What **Life Interests** and **Character Traits** describe you? What **Personal Style** do you bring to who you are? What **Aptitudes and Skills** do you possess? What **True Values** guide you.

Then you will look for your *joy*, beginning with listing your wants or external values. What work situation is a good fit for you, including **Work Environment** and **Preferred Employer**? What are your **Roles and Goals**? You will define your **Life Purpose** and **Dream Work** and then develop a **Life Purpose Statement** following the *be, do, have* paradigm that will be your guiding principles in setting a plan into motion.

We also have you collect all the relevant information and documents regarding your work history on what we refer to as "**Gathering Pages**." You will probably find that your former choices will be the building blocks for your future. You will conclude with developing your **Career Plan** and a **Work Template**, so you will be clear when you find the right opportunity or place, or maybe just so you will know that you are already in the right place. All this information becomes your **Living Career Portfolio** and your opportunity to take responsibility for your career and your work.

Why Build a Portfolio?

What better way to illustrate the art of your work life than to borrow a tool from the world of art and design? In today's work world, it is not enough to have an up-to-date resumé. The act of completing a resumé does little to inspire you into action, and sometimes it actually accomplishes quite the opposite. Building your portfolio walks you through the process of discovery, with the process being greater than the product itself. In addition, the portfolio represents a state-of-the-art approach to career management and design.

How Does the Process Work?

At the beginning of each chapter is an explanation of the content and its importance to your work life. We recommend that you proceed through the book in chronological order because the system we created deliberately builds upon the preceding work.

In addition to the actual exercises, you will be asked to respond to some coaching questions on the **Analysis and Reflection** pages. Through our coaching work, we have found that our clients' responses to these questions will provide additional insight and discovery. Thus, to accomplish this without a coach, we have included these pages after each exercise. While the questions may seem redundant at times, we encourage you to recognize their value and respond to them.

An ideal method for managing and organizing your portfolio is to use a binder as a repository for all the information you gather. In some cases, our clients have copied or removed pages from their book and filed them in their binder so that all their information was in one book. However you choose to organize your work, remember that it is a living process, so it will grow and change over time. As you become familiar with it, you will adapt it to your own situation.

You will periodically want to update your work. This is part of the process to keep your information current and relevant. We recommend that you view your portfolio as a "living" document. It is meant to be updated periodically and remain with you for the rest of your life.

How Will a Portfolio Work for You?

There are many career and employment related books that will tell you how to prepare a resumé and have it work for you. We believe that once you have completed our process, you won't need anyone to teach you how to use it because it will be part of who you are. Your portfolio can be used for job search or career advancement, but its greatest purpose is to help you connect with your motivation.

Our process will undoubtedly make you uncomfortable at times. Growth can be uncomfortable, as is seeing parts of ourself that are not normally in our view. You may experience a "significant emotional event," which can come in the form of an "aha" or an "ouch," i.e. seeing something about yourself that makes you uncomfortable. When a significant amount of energy is expended, any person will become vulnerable just from the exertion, never mind adding the vulnerability that comes along with scrutinizing yourself in the process. This process is designed to recognize your strengths and to identify what it is that causes your blockages. It is a fact that when examining anything, the object of examination changes just by being exposed to the process of observation. And change is difficult, no matter how ready we are for it. So be gentle with yourself and respect the undertaking you are committing to.

"Sometimes the most important thing you learn is what you already know."

— Bob

*"I am not what I think I am,
I am not what you think I am,
I am what I think you think I am ..."*

— Unknown

"What lies behind us and what lies before us are tiny matters compared to what lies within us."

— Ralph Waldo Emerson

What Is Your Story?

Where Are You?

This is your opportunity to look at your current reality, how you have gotten here, and what you *believe* the choices are in your present situation. This is the first step in identifying the building blocks and potential barriers that exist in your work life, and it is where you will find your power. It is important to sort out what the issues are so you can develop a strategy that promotes action and enables you to manage the options in your present circumstances with clarity. Along the way, you will decide what you can and can't live with. The more you understand what is important to you, the better chance you have to work in a job and an environment that will invigorate you and provide you with the opportunities for success and fulfillment

Assessing your current reality and needs will also guide you in achieving balance in your life, relative to your interests, priorities and relationships. You will begin to identify the raw material that makes up who you are — material that you will continue to work with throughout the process of creating your portfolio. Yet it is valuable to reexamine these aspects of your life periodically, because they will shift and change. As you revisit the exercises in this book, your portfolio will grow and transform with you, so that it will be a viable tool at any point in your life.

To identify your current relationship with work, you will be completing the following exercises:

- **Work Health Assessment**
  This series of questions will help you identify the realities of every aspect of employment, including career choices, relationships, satisfaction, personal status, pending transitions, self-development, self-marketing and many other characteristics of a job situation. You will complete a personal checkup to determine in which areas you need to focus on to improve the current state of your career and provide motivation while you work through the activities in this book.

- **Your Stories**
  This exercise helps you to summarize where you have been, how you have seen yourself, what you remember, what you have accomplished, and what you have seen as obstacles in your life. The answers to these questions are the most important clues to who you authentically are and how you experience joy. This exercise will prompt you to explore your life in terms of stories that represent the different stages of your life. You will be using these stories throughout the book as the basis for investigating your traits, style, skills, aptitudes and values, and to formulate what it is that you really want.

- **Life Facets**
  This exercise will help you identify which areas of your life are the most important to you and how much time you spend in those areas. It is a reality check: Do your activities match with what you *say* is truly important to you? This exercise will give you the opportunity to think about your current choices and how they align with what you desire. You will consider how to begin to use message number four of the five key messages, "Life is full of trade-offs," and you will learn to recognize which choices elicit joy and which ones you choose to let go.

- **Life Purpose**
  Some of the most passionate questions a person asks of their life include, "What is my purpose?" "What am I here for?" and "How does my life have meaning?" And the answers are some of the hardest for people to discover. This exercise begins the process of developing your Life Purpose Statement for ***being***. In later chapters, you will continue formulating your purpose by exploring your ***doing***, and then what you want to ***have***. You will be putting all this information together to formulate a Life Purpose Statement in chapter 6.

Work Health Assessment

How healthy is your career? What would help improve the overall quality of your work life? Where can you start? The Work Health Assessment is designed to examine all aspects of your work life and career. It will at least confirm what you already know about yourself and your work. At best, it will identify opportunities for you to "get into action" to find your power.

You may feel you already know what, if any, issues you are dealing with regarding your career or work life. You might even be able to pinpoint what aspects you want to work on, or what you believe would need to change in order to help you. That is great! However, we still encourage you to take the Work Health Assessment and further explore your work life in its entirety.

As you begin the questions on the following pages, remember that a "job" is the "work" associated with who you are, the *"doing"* part of your being. Typically your job is what you spend the majority of your time *doing*, whether it is a paid or unpaid activity. Examples of unpaid activity can be that of a retiree, parent, homemaker or even student. Keep these comments in mind if you do not think "job" pertains to you as you answer the questions (even if your answers focus on the fact that your "job" is to look for a job).

As you answer the questions, you will begin to see patterns emerging. Patterns refer to behaviors, thought processes, attitudes and interactions, basically — your way of *being* in the world. A pattern can serve us, contributing to our success and happiness, or it can hurt us and keep us from achieving joy in our work life.

Sometimes it is hard to recognize patterns. That is when a coach can be particularly helpful. Keep in mind you can also go to www.beingatwork.com and elect to fill out the first part of this questionnaire online, receiving automated coaching feedback on your blockages or gaps, and where you should focus your attention. You can also make arrangements to have the complete assessment analyzed by going to www.marybrandon.com. You may also find it useful to review your answers with a helping professional, mentor or friend.

Instructions: The following statements describe your current work situation. If you *agree* more than you disagree with a statement, place a check mark in the Y box for yes. If you *disagree* more than you agree with a statement, place a check mark in the N box for no.

It is preferable that you not rush through these questions, but consciously think them through. Recognize that no statement will be true for you 100 percent of the time. Remember that these questions are designed to cause you to reflect on your work life and personal situation, not to produce a "score" or slot you into some descriptive category.

If a particular question causes you to question yourself more deeply, note the thoughts you had in the space provided at the end of the questionnaire, or document your thoughts in a journal so that you can refer to them later.

Part A

Y N

☐ ☐ 1. I am happy in my present job and organization.
☐ ☐ 2. I am happy with what I *do*, but am less satisfied with where and with whom I *do* it.
☐ ☐ 3. My relationships at work are honest, respectful and safe.
☐ ☐ 4. I recognize what motivates me.
☐ ☐ 5. I recognize and can describe my strengths and weaknesses.
☐ ☐ 6. My job aligns with my interests.
☐ ☐ 7. I feel I don't spend my time on what is important to me.
☐ ☐ 8. I have values by which I make my decisions.
☐ ☐ 9. My work relates to the meaning of my life.
☐ ☐ 10. I do not feel that all my skills, abilities and talents are expressed in my life.
☐ ☐ 11. I am unwilling to make trade-offs between my personal life and my work.
☐ ☐ 12. I have a complete list of my employment history, including dates, addresses, job descriptions and accomplishments.
☐ ☐ 13. I am unhappy with the work style of my present organization.
☐ ☐ 14. The roles I play in my personal life are in alignment with my goals.
☐ ☐ 15. I don't like to work, but it is something I have to *do*.
☐ ☐ 16. I am clear about my goals and have plans for the future.
☐ ☐ 17. My work style is not the same as my personal style.
☐ ☐ 18. My values are in alignment with my current job, employer and colleagues.
☐ ☐ 19. My job is just a means to an end.
☐ ☐ 20. My aptitudes and skills are recognized at work.
☐ ☐ 21. I am not satisfied with my present job, but don't want a change.
☐ ☐ 22. What I have to *do* often conflicts with who I am.
☐ ☐ 23. I recognize the influences in my life and the impact on what I *do*.
☐ ☐ 24. I have values which conflict with my job satisfaction.
☐ ☐ 25. I am preparing for a major change in what I *do*, such as changing careers or retiring.
☐ ☐ 26. I can *succinctly* describe my major accomplishments.
☐ ☐ 27. I am prepared to pursue other opportunities at any given moment.
☐ ☐ 28. I am presently unemployed and am very fearful about finding work.
☐ ☐ 29. I fear losing my job.
☐ ☐ 30. What I have in my life is not what I want.
☐ ☐ 31. I recognize my marketable skills.
☐ ☐ 32. I have to sacrifice my interpersonal style to get along with my colleagues and superiors.
☐ ☐ 33. I am on a path to achieve my dream job.
☐ ☐ 34. I am not who people at work think I am.

Part B

Instructions: The following are options that you *could* consider in your current work situation. Place a check mark if you *would* consider this option.

___I would stay in the *same* job in the *same* organization.

___I would stay in the *same* job in a *different* organization.

___I would find a *different* job in the *same* organization.

___I would find a *different* job in a *different* organization.

___Other. I would _____

_____

_____

Part C

Instructions: The following are factors that may be impacting your work life. If you *agree* more than you disagree with a statement, place a check mark in the Y box for yes. If you *disagree* more than you agree, place a check mark in the N box for no.

Y N

☐☐ 1. Interpersonal conflicts are affecting my morale.

☐☐ 2. I work with individuals or with an organization whose values conflict with mine.

☐☐ 3. I have tried everything I can and cannot resolve issues at work.

☐☐ 4. The work I *do* does not align with my life purpose.

☐☐ 5. I am a much different person at work than I am in my personal life.

☐☐ 6. What I am being asked to *do* at work is not what I want to *do*.

☐☐ 7. I am not aware of what options are available to me to advance my career.

☐☐ 8. I do not know my next career move.

☐☐ 9. I am feeling stuck in my job.

☐☐ 10. I don't know how to get ahead.

☐☐ 11. I have no one to consult with on problems I encounter.

☐☐ 12. I need to gain more experience to be successful.

☐☐ 13. I am experiencing too many periods of instability.

☐☐ 14. My physical health is being impacted by changes at work.

☐☐ 15. I find it difficult to deal with change.

☐☐ 16. I am not paid what I am worth.

☐☐ 17. I need a raise.

☐☐ 18. I asked for a raise but didn't get it.

☐☐ 19. I am currently unemployed.

☐☐ 20. I am not happy with my current job, my work environment, or a person or people at work.

☐☐ 21. I plan to undertake a job search, but I don't know how to go about it.

☐☐ 22. I have a work goal, but haven't achieved it.

☐☐ 23. When I have more than one choice, I have a hard time deciding which choice is right for me.

☐☐ 24. It is easier for me to know whether a decision is right or wrong if someone else makes it.

Y N

☐ ☐ 25. I totally agree with and understand the feedback on my evaluations.
☐ ☐ 26. I feel my present job is a dead end.
☐ ☐ 27. I am not sure what developmental options are open to me.
☐ ☐ 28. There is so much for me to *do*, it is hard to know where to begin.
☐ ☐ 29. There is no time to do the things that I *have* to *do*, let alone the things that I *want* to *do*.
☐ ☐ 30. I don't know what I want.
☐ ☐ 31. I am not supported in what I really want to *do*.
☐ ☐ 32. I don't know how to ask the people in my life to support my goals.
☐ ☐ 33. I don't know anyone who can help me.
☐ ☐ 34. I worry about money a lot.
☐ ☐ 35. I would like to change careers or retire, but don't know if I can afford to *do* that.
☐ ☐ 36. My current job does not pay me enough money to meet my expenses.
☐ ☐ 37. My answers in an interview will get me the job.
☐ ☐ 38. The goal of an interview is to see if I can get them to like me.
☐ ☐ 39. The person who is conducting the interview is in charge.
☐ ☐ 40. I haven't received a performance evaluation recently.
☐ ☐ 41. I disagree with my leader's assessment of my strengths and weaknesses.
☐ ☐ 42. Others are unhappy with my work performance or commitment.
☐ ☐ 43. I have no power or input in managing my job.
☐ ☐ 44. I find it difficult to get excited about my job.
☐ ☐ 45. I do not know how my job fits into the overall organization.
☐ ☐ 46. I feel that I am often not heard.
☐ ☐ 47. I am often misunderstood when I attempt to communicate with others.
☐ ☐ 48. My work relationships are less than desirable.
☐ ☐ 49. I don't like to promote myself or know where to begin.
☐ ☐ 50. My performance is not recognized and I am not acknowledged.
☐ ☐ 51. I don't think getting a new position, or advancement, is a matter of promoting myself.
☐ ☐ 52. I have a problem identifying where my job needs improvement.
☐ ☐ 53. I have a problem identifying what training or education is needed to enhance my job.
☐ ☐ 54. My job description does not match what I am *doing*.
☐ ☐ 55. I was terminated unfavorably and feel uncomfortable with giving references.
☐ ☐ 56. I don't know anyone who would give me a reference.
☐ ☐ 57. I have no work experience, so I do not have any references.
☐ ☐ 58. I would like to start planning for my retirement.
☐ ☐ 59. I am worried that I may be forced to retire.
☐ ☐ 60. I have been offered an incentive to retire, but don't know if I should accept it.
☐ ☐ 61. I am getting ready to retire.

Y N

- [ ] [ ] 62. I don't have any plans for retirement.
- [ ] [ ] 63. My work is the primary focus of my life, and I don't know what I am going to **do** when I retire.
- [ ] [ ] 64. I have some excellent skills that are not being used in my job.
- [ ] [ ] 65. I would like some additional training to increase my skills.
- [ ] [ ] 66. I am fearful that my skills are inadequate for my job.
- [ ] [ ] 67. My present work skills do not match the career I prefer.
- [ ] [ ] 68. I don't think I have any transferable skills.
- [ ] [ ] 69. I would like to enter the workforce after **being** out of it for some time, or I have never held a formal job.
- [ ] [ ] 70. I am looking for a new job and haven't used my network.
- [ ] [ ] 71. I put together a list of individuals that could help me in a job search, and there were less than ten people on it.
- [ ] [ ] 72. I don't know what a network is, or what value it would be to me.
- [ ] [ ] 73. I don't like my current position and don't know why.
- [ ] [ ] 74. I get frustrated with the way my company is run.
- [ ] [ ] 75. I am looking for a new position and don't want to make a mistake.
- [ ] [ ] 76. I have recently lost my job or had a career disappointment.
- [ ] [ ] 77. My position does not look like it will be needed in the future, and I am "paralyzed."
- [ ] [ ] 78. Things have changed noticeably in my company, job or life, and I am having difficulty coping.
- [ ] [ ] 79. There are many things and people that demand my time and attention.
- [ ] [ ] 80. I am in a no-win situation.
- [ ] [ ] 81. If I could identify the problem, I would fix it.
- [ ] [ ] 82. I am too old to get hired.
- [ ] [ ] 83. I am **being** discriminated against.
- [ ] [ ] 84. I need special accommodations to perform my job adequately.
- [ ] [ ] 85. I would like to have more self-confidence, and I frequently feel inferior to others.
- [ ] [ ] 86. I feel or have been told that my physical appearance is interfering with my career.
- [ ] [ ] 87. I feel my physical stamina interferes with my job.
- [ ] [ ] 88. I feel I lack education, or the kind of education I received is inadequate.
- [ ] [ ] 89. I have a college degree, but wonder if I should consider a post-graduate degree.
- [ ] [ ] 90. I am not working in my college major.
- [ ] [ ] 91. I don't have a current resumé.
- [ ] [ ] 92. My resumé is not getting results.
- [ ] [ ] 93. My resumé does not adequately reflect my goals.
- [ ] [ ] 94. I believe my personal values are being challenged at work.
- [ ] [ ] 95. I often don't agree with my colleagues or their approach to work.
- [ ] [ ] 96. I don't feel that I fit in at my current organization.

Write down any work challenges not already identified that are disturbing you.

___

Now that you have completed the Work Health Assessment, what would you most like to accomplish or improve while you work through the process of completing this book and your own portfolio? What changes would you like to see that would serve as evidence that completing these activities has been time well spent?

___

Additional comments:

___

Work Health Assessment – Analysis and Reflection

Instructions: These are coaching questions, a means of reflecting on this exercise for greater insight. We recommend you review them and write down your thoughts.

1. What did you learn were the best aspects, or areas of contentment, in your current situation?

2. What did you learn were the worst aspects, or areas of dissatisfaction, in your current situation?

3. What insights did you gain, or are you having difficulty with gaining any insight?

4. Did any of the questions trigger an emotional response, such as anxiety, sadness, anger, frustration or fear?

5. Do you see a theme beginning to emerge? What conclusion, if any, can you presently make about your situation? How do the issues relate to each another?

6. If you had the authority to change your current work situation, what changes would you make?

Your Stories

*"Character is what is forged by the fire of our past.
The imprint it leaves upon us is what we bring to our future."*

—Mary

There are countless stories about human character that so impress us that we do not easily forget them. There is the story of Albert Einstein, one of the greatest thinkers of our time, who had difficulty in school and almost failed, but went on to discover the theory of relativity, altering the way we view space and time. A story about Winston Churchill blamed him for one of the greatest military defeats in British history at Gallipoli, yet he went on to become a heroic prime minister during World War II. Churchill called the period after his Gallipoli experience his "years in the wilderness." What impact did these stories have on their character and future success, and what do they reveal about both men?

As you may have realized, it is often difficult to look at ourself and honestly answer questions related to our ***being***. We have found the stories of our past to be a useful tool to help identify various aspects of who we are. These stories are also indicators of who we will be in the future. Writing such stories provides our mind with another framework to use for gaining insight. You will be using your own stories in a variety of exercises throughout this book.

The stories we are asking you to write are those about your **proudest moments, major accomplishments** or **significant events** in your life **that stand out to you**, for whatever reason; in other words, those times when you had a real sense of happiness and well-being, or times that are so significant to the development, and therefore expression, of your character. You will start with the beginning of your life. We have organized this exercise in five year increments as a *suggested* outline to help you formulate your thoughts. The point is to write about a variety of time frames and circumstances so that you have enough information from which to draw. If you have a time frame where a lot of significant events happened, feel free to express them. It may be hard to remember your early years, however this is a meaningful time. As children, we tend to be unencumbered by societal mores and demands, and often these memories are more reflective of our true being. Another technique is to interview others who knew you as a child or remember stories about you. Don't second-guess yourself or over analyze your memories. Trust that whatever you are writing contains the necessary information.

It is best to undertake this exercise when you can devote the time, as it is the backbone for completing subsequent exercises throughout the book. It is okay to skip around, and once you are in the process, more memories will come to you. What is important is to write *something* down for each time frame. When you have completed the assignment, walk away from it to see if anything else comes to mind, and if so, add to what you have written.

One final thought. Many of us are used to doing our writing on a computer. While this is efficient, it is not as conducive to the creative process. We recommend that you write your stories in longhand. Because of the flow of cursive writing, you may experience more creative releases. Give it a try. If the space we have allowed on the following pages is not enough, use it for notes and use a journal to more freely express and organize your thoughts. We have also provided examples of our stories, to inspire you to write and further acquaint you with us, *your coaches*!

Instructions: Write your story, starting with birth to 5 year of age, 5 to 10 years of age, 10 to 15 years of age, and so on. Focus on the following points to help prompt your thoughts:

- ★ **Proudest moments**
- ★ **Major accomplishments**
- ★ **Significant life events**

Here are examples of our stories:

A story from Mary
5 to 10 years of age

During third grade recess, I approached a crying girl standing alone on the school playground. She was being taunted and teased, and deliberately excluded from playing with the other children. I had just moved to this new school. At my last school, my companionship was sought after. I had not yet experienced rejection like this girl was facing. I decided that day how I wanted to be in my relationships and recognized how important equitable treatment for all people was to me. From that moment on, we became the best of friends, together navigating imposed isolation and judgment. We remain deeply connected to this day.

A story from Prudence
20 to 25 years of age

In my last year of college, I started talking with some friends about backpacking through Europe. When the departure time drew close, they had to cancel. I still wanted to go, so I went by myself. To make the trip possible, I had to save my money, research places in Europe I wanted to see, plan my itinerary, purchase a Eurail pass and plane ticket. I backpacked through Europe for two months and had an incredible time. In retrospect, I am amazed at my guts to do this.

A story from Bob
15 to 20 years of age

When I graduated from high school at the age of 18, I joined the Marine Corps. A year later, I was sent to Korea, where I participated in six major combat engagements in 10 months. I was one of 19 survivors of 56 men in a machine gun platoon during the Chosin Reservoir campaign, when our division was surrounded by 10 Chinese divisions. As a result, I was promoted to corporal. This was an early promotion and the first of many during the 28 years I would serve as a Marine.

Your Stories

Birth to 5 years of age

5 to 10 years of age

10 to 15 years of age

15 to 20 years of age

20 to 25 years of age

25 to 30 years of age

30 to 35 years of age

35 to 40 years of age

40 to 45 years of age

45 to 50 years of age

50 to 55 years of age

55 to 60 years of age
_____
_____
_____
_____

60 to 65 years of age
_____
_____
_____
_____

65 to 70 years of age
_____
_____
_____
_____

70 to 75 years of age
_____
_____
_____
_____

75 to 80 years of age
_____
_____
_____
_____

80 plus years of age
_____
_____
_____
_____

Your Stories – Analysis and Reflection

Instructions: These are coaching questions, a means of reflecting on this exercise for greater insight. We recommend you review them and write down your thoughts.

1. **What type of stories did you tend to remember and write about?**

2. **What reaction did you have to writing your stories? Did you feel frustration, sadness, happiness, joy, excitement, anger, or other emotions?**

3. **What was the biggest obstacle in writing your stories?**

4. **Do you see any themes or patterns emerging from your stories?**

5. **What were your favorite stories, and why?**

6. **What were your least favorite stories, and why?**

Life Facets

A reporter was interviewing millionaire J. Paul Getty one day in his office in downtown Manhattan. The reporter looked out the window and saw a beggar sitting on the curb 10 stories below. He turned to Mr. Getty and asked, "Mr. Getty, what is the difference between you and that beggar sitting down there on the curb?" Getty thought for a moment and replied, "The way we use our time."

Is your use of time a conscious choice, or does it simply just "happen"? The Life Facets exercise is an opportunity to take a look at the dynamics of life through how you choose to use your time. Time is our most precious commodity, with many people feeling there are not enough hours in a day to do what they *have* to do, let alone what they *want* to do. Time can be our biggest motivator, but it is not forgiving. It doesn't care whether we are conscious of how we spend it, or whether we are clear on the consequences, it just keeps moving forward, taking a little bit of our life with it.

In this exercise, you will analyze the importance of each category of time and then assess how you actually use it. Are your priorities easy? Do they feed you with energy, or do they leave you less than fulfilled? The intent is to have you analyze what you must do to take responsibility for what you want, and who you will be while accomplishing it.

We only have 24 hours in a day. We can't save or store time, we have to "use it or lose it." How we choose to spend time is yet another demonstration of who we are. In some cases, you may have to make changes in how you spend your time if you want to achieve the goals you set. You may want to assess whether you like the stories that will develop with these particular priorities in your life.

What Is Your Story?

Instructions: Begin by reading over the definitions of the Life Facets. Then, in the left-hand column, with the heading "Priority," rank the Life Facets in the order of their importance to you at this time in your life. Number 1 would be the most important, and number 8 would be the least important.

In the right-hand column, with the heading "Time," rank each area in order of approximately how much time you actually spend in that area in an average day, week or month (your choice). Consider number 1 as the most time spent and number 8 as the least time spent. Note: In each column, you may have only one of each number, 1 through 8, with no ties allowed.

Priority	Life Facets	Time
	Work/Career — What you do to make a living and meet your need for self-satisfaction and self-esteem. Your job, including all aspects of the job.	
	Personal Relations — Your relationships with your family, friends, relatives, neighbors, fellow workers, and other people with whom you interact.	
	Health and Fitness — The things you do to keep your physical body fit and healthy, such as exercise, proper eating and drinking habits, sleep, annual physical, etc.	
	Personal Growth — The things you do to improve your mind and increase your knowledge to help you function, survive, and live better. Includes reading, listening to self-improvement tapes, taking classes, etc.	
	Spiritual — The things you do to help your inner self grow and understand your relationship with the universe, the source of your inner strength, power, beliefs and values. Attending church, temple, or synagogue, praying, meditating, reading religious material, being in and contemplating the structure and harmony of nature, etc.	
	Citizenship — The things you do as a good citizen of the community in which you live, such as charitable contributions, volunteer activities, and being tolerant of diversity in society.	
	Economic — The things you do to manage your financial matters, such as paying bills, material purchases, saving and budgeting.	
	Play — The things you do to relax and have fun, including playing or watching your favorite games, reading a good book for relaxation, or other forms of entertainment.	

Life Facets – Analysis and Reflection

Instructions: These are coaching questions, a means of reflecting on this exercise for greater insight. We recommend you review them and write down your thoughts.

1. Were there any surprises when you compared your priorities with your use of time? How were you, or were you not, surprised?

2. How are your priorities a reflection of you and what you want?

3. What do you believe about the balances or imbalances between your priorities and how you spend time?

4. What trade-offs would you have to make (or have already made), in either your priorities or time spent, that leave you feeling disappointed?

5. What did you determine is important, as well as not important to you, through this exercise?

6. How would you like to change your priorities? Be as specific as you can.

Life Purpose

Were you surprised by your results in the Life Facets? Were you happy with them? Now how would you respond to the question, "Are you living on purpose?" Whether you consider the question one of intention or volition, knowing you are living on purpose is to understand your reason for *being*. When we live on purpose, the world opens up to us and our lives take on new meaning.

To define your purpose, your reason for *being*, is to define your compass. It provides the opportunity to align your work so that it is in harmony with your deepest values, beliefs and strengths. It simplifies your life because you now know what to do. You are able to make decisions consistent with your purpose, acknowledging your unique talents, allocating your time, and using your resources in a way that brings you joy.

Often people go in search of their purpose as if it were "out there" somewhere, waiting to be discovered, but as elusive as the Holy Grail. To recognize that the clues for your purpose are within you is the first step toward clarity. Clarity and meaning go hand in hand when you discover yourself one step at a time. As Rick Warren states in *The Purpose Driven Life*, "Nothing energizes like a clear purpose. On the other hand, passion dissipates when you lack purpose . . . It is usually meaningless work, not overwork, that wears us down, saps our strength, and robs our joy."

Finding your purpose takes time and reflection. The following questions have been designed as the beginning of this process. *They are designed to start you thinking about life and what it is all about for you.* Later, in chapters 3, 4 and 5, you will work on the *being, doing* and *having* aspect of your life purpose, culminating in your Life Purpose Statement.

Instructions: The following are some intriguing questions to start you thinking about your life purpose. Answer as many as you can.

List three things you would like to accomplish that would make you feel great.

What do you want others to say are your contributions?

How would you occupy your time if you were a billionaire?

List absorbing childhood activities you remember.

What would you do if it were impossible to fail?

What would you regret not having done if your life was ending now?

What are your daydreams, hopes and wishes?

How would you make the world better?

What character would you love to portray at a costume party?

List a dream job someone you know has?

Who is your number one role model, and why?

When does your body feel most "alive"?

What's an award you'd be proud to receive?

What book, movie or TV program character would you like to be?

If you had a day to do anything you wanted with no cares, judgments, etc., what would you do?

If you were to choose another name for yourself that was reflective of you, what would it be?

What things come easy, naturally and effortlessly to you?

Write your epitaph.

Life Purpose – Analysis and Reflection

Instructions: These are coaching questions, a means of reflecting on this exercise for greater insight. We recommend you review them and write down your thoughts.

1. What questions had the biggest impact on you? Why?

2. What did you learn about yourself in doing this exercise?

3. Do you feel you have been living with some kind of purpose? How conscious or deliberate does that appear?

4. How would you describe what that purpose currently looks like?

5. What similarities or patterns emerged from your answers?

6. What could you do right now to move closer to living your life on purpose, consistent with what you have discovered thus far?

"To thine own self be true."

— William Shakespeare

"Seek first to understand and then to be understood."

— Stephen Covey

Know Thyself 3

Who Are You?

"The term "Walkabout" comes from the Australian Aboriginal. The idea is that a person can get so caught up in one's work, obligations and duties that the truly important parts of one's self become lost. From there it is a downward spiral as one gets farther and farther from the true self. A crisis situation usually develops that awakens the wayward to the absent true self.

It is at this time that one must go on walkabout. All possessions are left behind (except for essential items) and one starts walking. Metaphorically speaking, the journey goes on until you meet yourself. Once you find yourself, you sit down and have a long talk about what one has learned, felt and done in each other's absence. One talks until there is nothing left to say—the truly important things cannot be said. If one is lucky, after everything has been said and unsaid, one looks up and sees only one person instead of the previous two." (Sean Connolly, nomad4@gonewalkabout.com, 2002)

Let's continue on with your discovery of yourself. Have you ever wondered why some people tend to disturb you, while others seem more in tune with you? When this occurs, you may be experiencing a difference in traits and styles that is causing friction. For example, take a manager who asks two of her employees the same question and waits for their response. The first employee sits there contemplating the question for a while, then answers the question. The second employee begins talking immediately, rambling a bit until he or she gives the answer to the question. One employee is stronger on the analytical (left-brain) side, possibly oriented to matters of intellect, or "head," while the other is stronger on the intuitive (right-brain) side, possibly oriented to matters social in nature, or "heart." This preference is associated with learning styles, which we will cover in more detail later in the chapter. Also, each employee possesses different traits, which are displayed while answering the question. If criticized by the manager on their answer, one may respond with a quick temper and a quick defense, while the other may look hurt and embarrassed, withdrawing and taking the matter very personally. In other words, we all have a preferred style of communication and interaction that is reinforced by certain traits we have developed over our lifetime.

Another aspect of recognizing ourselves is that it is the key to connecting and relating to others. To understand this is to begin learning how to work better with the people we interface with daily.

Assessments Versus Observations
To do this work, you will need to take your opinions and feelings into account, and yet remain objective. Try to become an observer of yourself and avoid making assessments. Assessments are subjective, while observations are factual. We ask you to try to curtail your assessments and focus on the facts of who you are.

The exercises in this chapter are about taking the time to come face-to-face with yourself by asking questions and searching for the answers that are true for you. You will begin by observing your interests, identifying your traits, and appraising the components of your style. Be careful to stay focused on your goal to discover the real you. Remember, sometimes it is through observing our greatest weaknesses that we can see our true gifts.

The Whole is Greater Than the Sum of the Parts
As you complete the exercises in this chapter, keep in mind that all of these areas are interrelated. You have developed traits as a result of your perceived needs for survival. Family and culture, as well as biology and physical makeup, have also influenced your traits. Style is often thought of as tendencies with which we were born, and it is a *natural* way for us to organize our traits.

Our goal for this chapter is for you to begin to recognize who you *consciously* prefer to "**be**," and accept who you are.

- **Life Interests**
  This exercise is designed to get you to understand what your interests are and how your work aligns with those interests, which is critical for achieving the power to create *joy* in work. Imagine spending all your work life doing something that holds no interest for you. This is not an uncommon situation.

  There are two parts to this exercise. First, you will work with characteristics and behaviors, and see how they translate into categories of interests. Second, you will be exploring the stories you wrote, paying particular attention to what you did as a child.

- **Character Traits**

  Think of traits as those characteristics that describe you and your behavior. Traits describe, in a sense, the demeanor with which you do everything. Psychologists believe our traits, along with our intellect or ability, determine job performance. Traits are developed as a way to cope with the world. Again, using Your Stories, you will identify the Character Traits you developed, notice how they have served you, and assess whether they are still useful to you now.

- **Personal Style**

  Your Personal Style is the overall way you *do* things, and that you will identify by examining Your Stories. You will begin by looking at sets of traits that make up an archetype (character), and then the motivators or needs you have attempted to fill in your life.

- **Putting It All Together**

  This exercise pulls together the work you have done in this chapter. You will start by examining the beliefs you hold regarding your Life Interests, Character Traits and Personal Style. You will then have an opportunity to question whether those beliefs are in your best interest. You will continue with finding your Life Purpose. This is the first exercise in a series that will offer you the opportunity to *think big* about who you are. You will be using this information to formulate your Life Purpose Statement later in the book.

The Fun and the Warning in Using Categorization!

Much has been written about categorizing us relative to our interests, traits and style preferences. Traits and styles are categorized in assessments such as the Myers Briggs Personality Type Indicator, 16 personality types, the 12 signs of the zodiac, the four temperaments, three primary styles of learning, right brain/left brain, etc. Just take your pick and be assured that someone will find a new way of expressing preferences in the near future. Carl Jung advised however, that when doing self-assessment, we should not take this categorization business too seriously, such as using it for purposes of segregation, discrimination or labeling, because as Jung said, "…every individual is an exception to the rule." (Sharp 1987, 35). In our interpretation, categorizing individuals and groups can become destructive, so we caution that you first understand yourself before making judgments about someone else.

Life Interests

What brings you satisfaction? What do you do when you are free to choose? Have you ever experienced tiredness and annoyance when getting out of bed for work, and then on weekends bounded out of bed totally energized and excited about the day? You feel the latter when your "doing" is in alignment with your interests.

What does it take for you to feel happy, to find joy in your work? Ultimately, it is about your interests, or doing what you like to do. Your interests have been with you since you were a child. Asking people to remember what they did as a child will demonstrate that when we are free to choose, we choose that which interests us. You might say that your Life Interests are at a soul level, long-held and emotionally driven passions.

It is clearly a gift when work aligns with interests. When we talk about this level of interest we are referring to what Timothy Butler and James Waldroop called "deeply embedded" life interests in their article "Job Sculpting: The Art of Retaining Your Best People." We have witnessed individuals whose work tapped into their abilities, allowing them to utilize skills which encompass their knowledge and experience. We have also worked with individuals who achieved the values or the rewards being sought, but there was little sense of power, and no apparent passion or joy because work did not tap into their interests. The level at which our work connects with our interests shows up in the results we produce, in the success we achieve, and in the ultimate value we bring to our employer. Would your employer or colleagues say you had passion, enthusiasm, creativity, energy and happiness surrounding your work?

We will use two exercises to examine your life interests. In Part A, we adapted the findings of Butler and Waldroop from their career development research (Butler and Waldroop 1999,144-152). Their work identified eight "deeply embedded" interests for people drawn to business careers. They note, "…most people in business are motivated by between one and three deeply embedded life interests – long-held, emotionally driven passions for certain kinds of activities. Deeply embedded interests are not hobbies or enthusiasms; they are innate passions that are intricately entwined with personality." Even if you are not employed in the business sector, you can demonstrate these interests.

Part B will have you look back on the stories in chapter 2. Your Stories, particularly those from your childhood, can reveal many of your Life Interests. First, because you remember them, they had some deep meaning for you, and second, we generally do what we like to do when we are young.

Life Interests - Part A

Instructions: Read through the eight groups of characteristics and behaviors. Place a check mark by each statement that describes you.

Group 1	Group 2
__You are intrigued by the inner workings of things. __You are curious about finding better ways to use technology to solve business problems. __You love the challenge of unlocking "codes." __You enjoy work that involves planning and analyzing production and operating systems. __You like to redesign business processes.	__You excel at working with numbers. __You see numbers and statistics as the best, and sometimes the only way to figure out business solutions. __You enjoy mathematical work and see it as fun. __You enjoy building computer models in order to determine optimal production scheduling and to perform accounting procedures. __You love analyzing customer research data versus the subjective findings of focus groups
Group 3	**Group 4**
__You enjoy thinking and talking about abstract ideas. __You find it exciting to build business models that would explain competition within a given industry. __You like analyzing the competitive position of a business within a particular market. __You are often drawn to academic work and subscribe to periodicals with an academic focus. __You are not only conversant in the language of theory, but also genuinely enjoy talking about abstract concepts.	__You enjoy the beginning of projects the most, when there are many unknowns and you can make something out of nothing. __You are frequently seen as imaginative, and an out-of-the-box thinker. __You seem most engaged when you are brainstorming or inventing unconventional solutions. __You thrive on newness. __You find satisfying work in new product development or advertising.

Group 5 __You enjoy teaching; in business this usually translates into coaching or mentoring. __You are driven to guide employees, peers and even clients to better performance. __You are drawn to work where you can help others improve. __You are often identified by your hobbies and volunteer for projects outside of work. __You are drawn to organizations that provide products or services you perceive to hold a high social value (i.e. museums, schools, hospitals).	**Group 6** __You want to manage people and enjoy dealing with them on a daily basis. __You derive a lot of satisfaction from workplace relationships, but you focus much more on outcomes. __You are interested in working with and through people to accomplish the goals of the business. __You have enjoyed or would enjoy a career in management or sales. __You have a strong desire to motivate, organize and direct people.
Group 7 __You are the happiest when running projects or teams. __You enjoy owning or being responsible for a transaction such as a trade or sale. __You like to have ultimate decision-making authority. __You feel great when in charge of making things happen. __You tend to ask for as much responsibility as possible in any work situation. __You are interested in deal making or in strategy; you would prefer being the CEO rather than the COO.	**Group 8** __You love expressing ideas for the sheer enjoyment that comes from storytelling, negotiating or persuading. __You love to influence people and projects through language and ideas. __You feel most fulfilled when writing, speaking or both. __You often volunteer for writing assignments. __You enjoy thinking about the audience.

Know Thyself

Instructions: After you have read through each group and selected all of the appropriate statements, <u>identify the one or two groups</u> which best represent your interests overall because you agree with the majority of their characteristics or behaviors. Then, review the group definitions that follow to learn more about how your interests are defined.

Definitions

Group 1	**Application of Technology** People who are intrigued by the inner workings of things, and who are curious about finding better ways to use technology to solve problems. They are analytical in nature, enjoy finding new ways to solve problems, and love the challenge of unlocking "codes."
Group 2	**Quantitative Analysis** People who excel at working with numbers. They see it as the best, and sometimes the only way to figure out solutions. They highly value logic and make assessments through cause and effect. They enjoy solving mathematical problems and working with numbers and statistics.
Group 3	**Theory Development and Conceptual Thinking** People who enjoy thinking and talking about abstract ideas. They can become excited by analyzing the competitive position within a particular market and building models that explain competition within a given industry. They subscribe to periodicals with an academic focus.
Group 4	**Creative Production** People who enjoy the beginning of a project most when there are many unknowns and they can make something out of nothing. These individuals are frequently seen as imaginative, out-of-the-box thinkers. They are especially interested in working on new product development or advertising campaigns to promote products, and can become frustrated when working on everyday tasks and repetitive situations.
Group 5	**Teaching, Counseling and Mentoring**. People who enjoy teaching will usually be seen as coaches or mentors in a non-school environment. These individuals get a lot of satisfaction guiding employees, peers and even clients to better performance. Focused on helping others, they often volunteer for activities outside of work.
Group 6	**Managing People and Relationships** People who want to manage people, and who enjoy dealing with people on a daily basis. They derive a lot of satisfaction from workplace relationships, but they focus much more on outcomes than do people in the counseling and mentoring category. They gravitate toward careers in management or sales.
Group 7	**Enterprise Control** People who are happiest when running projects or teams. They enjoy "owning" a transaction such as a trade or sale. They like to have ultimate decision-making authority. They feel great when they are in charge of making things happen. They take on as much responsibility for a project as possible and want to be in control.
Group 8	**Influence Through Language and Ideas** People who love expressing ideas for the sheer enjoyment that comes from storytelling, negotiating or persuading. They are people who like to talk or write about what they are thinking. They feel most fulfilled when they are writing, speaking or both.

Instructions: After reviewing the definitions for the one or two groups you selected, answer the follow questions.

    The Life Interests group/s I selected as being <u>most</u> aligned with my interests are _____.

    The Life Interests group/s I would select as <u>least</u> aligned with my interests are _____.

    In my current position, the work I do matches the Life Interests in group/s _____.

    Outside of work, I pursue activities that match the Life Interests in group/s _____.

    The Life Interests I selected (if any) that are not expressed in my current work, or activities outside work, are group/s _____.

Instructions: Now compare the groups you selected as being <u>most</u> and <u>least</u> aligned with your interests with those that are currently part of your life.

    What conclusions can you make?

Life Interests - Part B

Instructions: Now let's see what Your Stories in chapter 2 reveal about your interests. Review each story and identify the interest you were expressing. You are not limited to or have to use the group descriptions for Part A. Simply describe what you were happy doing.

Here is an example from Prudence's story about the backpacking trip to Europe, found on page 15.

20 to 25 years of age

My interests in this story were: *Travel, independently pursuing goals, doing what I wanted to do, power in taking control of the situation and doing it, planning, creating my own trip, deciding what I would see and where I would go, feeling excited about seeing new things, people and places.*

Birth to 5 years of age

My interests in this story were: _____

5 to 10 years of age

My interests in this story were: _____

10 to 15 years of age

My interests in this story were: _____
_____

15 to 20 years of age

My interests in this story were: _____
_____

20 to 25 years of age

My interests in this story were: _____
_____

25 to 30 years of age

My interests in this story were: _____
_____

30 to 35 years of age

My interests in this story were: _____
_____

35 to 40 years of age

My interests in this story were: _____
_____

40 to 45 years of age

My interests in this story were: _____
_____

45 to 50 years of age

My interests in this story were: _____
_____

50 to 55 years of age

My interests in this story were: _____
_____

55 to 60 years of age

My interests in this story were: _____
_____

60 to 65 years of age

My interests in this story were: _____
_____

65 to 70 years of age

My interests in this story were: _____
_____

70 to 75 years of age

My interests in this story were: _____
_____

75 to 80 years of age

My interests in this story were: _____
_____

80 plus years of age

My interests in this story were: _____
_____

Life Interests – Analysis and Reflection

Instructions: These are coaching questions, a means of reflecting on this exercise for greater insight. We recommend you review them and write down your thoughts.

1. What did you learn about the interests you have you demonstrated in your life?

2. Are there other interests you have which were not reflected in the Life Interests exercise or in Your Stories?

3. What insight did you gain regarding your interests?

4. Were there any interests identified that you feel you cannot presently pursue? Why?

5. What conclusions can you make about your interests and your work?

6. What change could you make right now to gain greater alignment with your interests?

Character Traits

Now that you have a sense of your Life Interests, we are going to take a look at your Character Traits. A trait is defined as a distinguishing feature of a person's character, or an inherited characteristic. Traits can describe our behavior towards others and how we act in a given situation.

We exhibit our Character Traits first and foremost in relationship to what we need. If a Character Trait works in achieving an expected result, we then believe it is the formula that will work to get our needs met. For example, if we learn when we are young that being cooperative keeps us safe, loved and cared for, which satisfies our physiological, survival, safety and belonging needs (Maslow 1988, p.53), we may apply that trait to our entire world, becoming a cooperative and accommodating adult. Of course you can see that there is strength in the trait of being cooperative, and there is also potential for weakness. The key is to understand which is which in a given situation, when to use it, and when not to use it. You can alter the use of your Character Traits consciously when you know yourself well enough.

The work you will do to identify your Character Traits has three parts. In Part A, you will review a list of traits to become familiar with what they are, and then select those that you see in yourself. There is also an opportunity to reflect on traits others might see in you. In Part B, you will look at whether these or any other Character Traits have shown up in Your Stories. Part C provides an opportunity to understand which Character Traits are serving you and which are not.

Character Traits - Part A

Instructions: Begin by becoming familiar with Character Traits. Read through the list and circle the words that describe you. Feel free to add to the list in the space provided at the bottom.

Character Traits

Honest	Fearful	Friendly
Light-hearted	Dependable	Adventurous
Leader	Anxious	Hard working
Expert	Courageous	Timid
Agreeable	Serious	Integrity
Conceited	Funny	Bold
Mischievous	Conservative	Daring
Demanding	Sad	Delicate
Thoughtful	Argumentative	Cooperative
Intense	Savvy	Lovable
Happy	Combative	Proper
Disagreeable	Selfish	Ambitious
Simple	Generous	Capable
Fair	Self-confident	Quiet
Caring	Respectful	Curious
Excitable	Considerate	Reserved

Studious	Imaginative	Pleasing
Inventive	Busy	Bossy
Creative	Patriotic	Witty
Thrilling	Fun-loving	Conscientious
Independent	Judgmental	Self-sacrificing
Intelligent	Shy	Energetic
Compassionate	Responsible	Cheerful
Gentle	Lazy	Athletic
Proud	Dreamer	Impulsive
Wild	Helpful	Loyal
Messy	Committed	Angry
Neat	Strong	Artistic
Driven	Insecure	Tough
Anxious	Humble	Organized

_____   _____   _____

_____   _____   _____

Instructions: A second opportunity regarding our Character Traits is to recognize how others perceive us. Take a second run-through of the list and put a check mark by those Character Traits you believe others would use to describe you.

Character Traits – Part B

Instructions: The next step is to go back and look at Your Stories in chapter 2. Try to do this part of the exercise by assuming that the person whose stories you are reviewing is not you, that you are merely an objective observer. Identify which Character Traits are reflected in each story. How would you objectively describe this person? What are their characteristics?

Here is an example from Bob's story as a young Marine, found on page 15.

15 to 20 years of age

The traits that I observe in this story are: *leader, proud, dependable, self-confident, patriotic, responsible, integrity, courageous, capable and conscientious.*

Birth to 5 years of age

The traits that I observe in this story are: _____

_____

5 to 10 years of age

The traits that I observe in this story are: _____
_____

10 to 15 years of age

The traits that I observe in this story are: _____
_____

15 to 20 years of age

The traits that I observe in this story are: _____
_____

20 to 25 years of age

The traits that I observe in this story are: _____
_____

25 to 30 years of age

The traits that I observe in this story are: _____
_____

30 to 35 years of age

The traits that I observe in this story are: _____
_____

35 to 40 years of age

The traits that I observe in this story are: _____
_____

40 to 45 years of age

The traits that I observe in this story are: _____
_____

45 to 50 years of age

The traits that I observe in this story are: _____
_____

50 to 55 years of age

The traits that I observe in this story are: _____
_____

55 to 60 years of age

The traits that I observe in this story are: _____
_____

60 to 65 years of age

The traits that I observe in this story are: _____
_____

65 to 70 years of age

The traits that I observe in this story are: _____
_____

70 to 75 years of age

The traits that I observe in this story are: _____
_____

75 to 80 years of age

The traits that I observe in this story are: _____
_____

80 plus years of age

The traits that I observe in this story are: _____
_____

Character Traits – Part C

Instructions: Now you have the opportunity to summarize what you have learned about your Character Traits. Review all of the traits you or others have identified and list the ten you feel serve you the best.

_____
_____
_____
_____
_____
_____
_____
_____
_____
_____

Instructions: Now identify any Character Traits which you feel do not serve you. Think about which traits tend to cause difficulties for others or you. Perhaps someone, such as a supervisor, colleague or partner, has made consistent comments about this trait being a problem for them, or you may be frustrated with a pattern that continues to repeat itself.

_____
_____
_____
_____

Character Traits – Analysis and Reflection

Instructions: These are coaching questions, a means of reflecting on this exercise for greater insight. We recommend you review them and write down your thoughts.

1. Were there any Character Traits represented in Your Stories that you did not circle or check?

2. Which Character Traits have served you well in your career or work life?

3. Are there any Character Traits you would like to abandon? Why or why not?

4. Which Character Traits do others see in you that you do not see in yourself?

5. Are there Character Traits you possess which you are not currently expressing?

6. A Character Trait that is a major predictor of job success is conscientiousness (responsible, dependable, organized and persistent). How do you or how could you express this trait?

Personal Style

Now you are going to examine your Personal Style. We have included this work because we have found an individual's style can be their greatest asset, as well as be their greatest liability. There is no right or wrong style. But it is valuable to recognize what you give up, ignore, or see as wrong because of your style. By recognizing your style, you have the opportunity to use it consciously in balance to further claim your power.

Your Personal Style is how you interact with the world and how you see and interpret what is going on. It is the way you have developed over the years to approach your work and your interactions with others. Every human being lives with the need to survive and thrive. Your Personal Style is an example of the choices your system has made in response to this either by nature or nurture.

Your style doesn't necessarily change, but the way you use it can, just as with your Character Traits. We often see the strongest of our traits and the extremes of how they are represented by observing our style when we are in crisis. In recognizing your Personal Style and understanding it, you will; 1.) become aware of how your style is unique to you; 2.) be better able to respect differences in others; 3.) be less apt to make wrong assumptions about others' behavior and needs; and 4.) build better relationships. All of these aspects are important to your work life.

Over the years, many tools have been used to identify styles. Our approach to assessing Personal Style is to work with the concept of archetypes identified by Carl Jung and later by authors such as Caroline Myss and Carol Pearson, who described various human commonalities that were consistent across cultures and times. This work is the basis for many personality assessment tools. The most common and frequently used is the Myers Briggs Personality Type Indicator.

You will use Your Stories to identify and analyze your Personal Style. Using your history may also help you recognize where a particular style was reinforced in your life. This can then allow you conscious choice about *how* you can use it.

In Part A, you will identify potential archetypes, that we will call characters, from a list. Think of these characters as describing a set of traits. Then in Part B, you will be introduced to motivators (also referred to as the needs you have) that influence your characters and thus your actions and choices. In Part C, you will analyze Your Stories for both the archetypes or characters represented, as well as what was motivating you, or the need you were expressing at the time. You will then summarize your findings to identify two of your Personal Styles. While it is helpful to understand your dominant style, it is more important to gain insight into the complicated way you react to different stimuli in different stages of your life.

This exercise takes the place of a traditional assessment tool pages 44-51 (The Legacy Technique ©Aspect Consulting 2001-2006) and is extensive. Give yourself time to complete it.

Personal Style – Part A

Archetypes have been used for centuries as a means of recognizing psychological patterns. A definition for archetype found at Dictionary.com:

> *An original model or type after which other similar things are patterned; a prototype: 'Frankenstein'... 'Dracula'... 'Dr. Jekyll and Mr. Hyde'... the archetypes that have influenced all subsequent horror stories" (New York Times).*

Know Thyself

An ideal example of a type; quintessence: an archetype of the successful entrepreneur.

In Jungian psychology, an inherited pattern of thought or symbolic imagery derived from the past collective experience and present in the individual unconscious.

In a similar manner to archetypes, we use the term *characters* as visual symbols to identify patterns of influence and common traits. These patterns give us clues to our belief system or the *strategies* we have put in place for relating to the world. These strategies can be inherent, something we are born with in our genetic coding or they are learned as we gain experience on how to respond to the world. Often we will assign traits and patterns to professions, economic classes, or even physical appearance in an attempt to make our world a little more predictable.

Instructions: Review this list of characters. Circle those that describe you. This is by no means a complete list, so feel free to add on to it at the bottom.

Characters

Innocent	Communicator	Mystic
Orphan	Politician	Healer
Bully	Inventor	Recluse
Clown	Leader	Angel
Child	Pirate	Lover
Dreamer	Scavenger	Caregiver
Saboteur	Seeker	Creator
Victim	Warrior	Destroyer
Prostitute	Ruler	Fool
Magician	Sage	Nurturer
Maiden	Detective	Muse
Robot	Extrovert	Loner
Visionary	Father	Grandmother
Follower	Patriarch	Artist
Seducer	Archer	Teacher
Slave	Hunter	Grandfather
Gambler	Scholar	Athlete
Manipulator	Producer	Actor
Gamer	Insect (choose one)	Counselor
Entrepreneur	Dictator	Animal (choose one)
Gardener	King	Cultivator
Addict	Queen	Alchemist
Rebel	Boss	Mother
Comedian	Decider	Servant
Princess	Master	Artisan
Prince	Provider	Martyr
Mentor	Liberator	Sensor
Matriarch	Advocate	Navigator
Knave	Pauper	_____
Naturalist	Pioneer	_____
_____	_____	_____
_____	_____	_____

Personal Style – Part B

Now we will look at what we call motivators. We all **do** things in a certain way based upon underlying needs. To become aware of your Personal Style, it is important to look at the needs you are expressing, and thus what is motivating you. Our needs reinforce how we act and demand attention through our entire life.

One way to look at needs is through the work of Abraham Maslow. Maslow stated that human needs are hierarchal, and pictured them in the form of a pyramid (Maslow 2000, p.1). The bottom of the pyramid deals with our survival, or physiological needs. The next levels are needs related to safety, then power and control, followed by esteem, love, and finally self-actualization, manifested actualization and transcendence. For the purposes of the following exercises, we will use his categories of needs while adding some of our own distinctions.

Instructions: Begin by becoming familiar with the list of needs we have referred to as motivators, and then address the questions that follow.

Motivators

8. Transcendence
Awareness, awakened, harmonized level of consciousness, not taking anything for granted, appreciation of diversity and simplicity, gaining information, wisdom and understanding, to be at peace and whole, transcending all other motivators.

7. Manifested Actualization
Intuition, visualization of the future, imagination, having a personal vision, manifesting your vision, manifesting synergy in a tangible way, being of service.

6. Self-Actualization
Expressed creativity, communication, connection, to hear and to be heard, living in the present, honoring the past in the foundation of the self, creating synergy.

5. Love
Acceptance, emotional expression, belonging, heart connection and compassion, unity and harmony, the balance of independence and dependence, forgiveness, responsibility, and authenticity.

4. Esteem
Attention, recognition, will, transformation, identity, self-esteem, power and control of self, desire for internal peace, ability to discern and maintain a personal sense of self, clear boundaries, ability to exist within a group and maintain one's sense of self.

3. Power and Control
Money or financial gain, relationships, sense of self-importance, status, expressed sexuality, worldly view of self, material power, success, pleasure, competency, creative process, and balance of responsibility.

2. Safety
Consistency, security, stability, predictability, material preservation, freedom from or elimination of crisis, security to allow letting go or moving on.

1. Physiological
Food, water, shelter, physical survival, maintaining a material existence, freedom to thrive, nurturing (touch) or physical attention.

Do you recognize any motivators you are currently answering to?

What motivators inspire you?

What motivators have you primarily operated from in your life?

Personal Style - Part C

Instructions: Now use what you learned about motivators and character and identify these aspects in each of Your Stories. You may begin to notice how intertwined they are. Notice that we have reversed the order of motivators and character in the exercise, versus how we initially presented them. It is easier to identify what was motivating you in Your Story first, and then see the characters that remind you of the person you were **being**.

You can use the list of characters on page 45 provided or you can create your own. In identifying the motivators, be sure to include both the name as well as the number of that level. If you wrote multiple stories for a time period, select the one you feel is most significant.

Here is an example from Mary's story of the girl on the playground, found on page 15.

5 to 10 years of age

The motivator I associate with this story is *Esteem #4*

The character I associate with this story is *The Innocent*

Birth to 5 years of age
The motivator I associate with this story is _____ # ____

The character I associate with this story is _____ # ____

5 to 10 years of age
The motivator I associate with this story is _____ # ____

The character I associate with this story is _____ # ____

10 to 15 years of age
The motivator I associate with this story is _____ # _____

The character I associate with this story is _____ # _____

15 to 10 years of age
The motivator I associate with this story is _____ # _____

The character I associate with this story is _____ # _____

20 to 25 years of age
The motivator I associate with this story is _____ # _____

The character I associate with this story is _____ # _____

25 to 30 years of age
The motivator I associate with this story is _____ # _____

The character I associate with this story is _____ # _____

30 to 35 years of age
The motivator I associate with this story is _____ # _____

The character I associate with this story is _____ # _____

35 to 40 years of age
The motivator I associate with this story is _____ # _____

The character I associate with this story is _____ # _____

40 to 45 years of age
The motivator I associate with this story is _____ # _____

The character I associate with this story is _____ # _____

45 to 50 years of age
The motivator I associate with this story is _____ # _____

The character I associate with this story is _____ # _____

50 to 55 years of age
The motivator I associate with this story is _____ # ____

The character I associate with this story is _____ # ____

55 to 60 years of age
The motivator I associate with this story is _____ # ____

The character I associate with this story is _____ # ____

60 to 65 years of age
The motivator I associate with this story is _____ # ____

The character I associate with this story is _____ # ____

65 to 70 years of age
The motivator I associate with this story is _____ # ____

The character I associate with this story is _____ # ____

70 to 75 years of age
The motivator I associate with this story is _____ # ____

The character I associate with this story is _____ # ____

75 to 80 years of age
The motivator I associate with this story is _____ # ____

The character I associate with this story is _____ # ____

80 plus years of age
The motivator I associate with this story is _____ # ____

The character I associate with this story is _____ # ____

Personal Style – Summary

Now let's look at what you found relative to your Personal Style.

Instructions: Look over the analysis of Your Stories and total the number of times you identified each motivator or need. In other words, count the number of stories where you were fulfilling a physiological need, then how many with a safety need, and so on, and fill in the total number of stories you had documented for that motivator. Then list the various characters that you identified for each motivator. Be patient, you are looking for patterns and strategies here. Once you are aware of the patterns or strategies you use, you can alter them by making deliberate or alternate choices.

Motivator	Total Occurrences	Characters
8. Transcendence	_____	_____
		_____
		_____
7. Manifested Actualization	_____	_____
		_____
		_____
6. Self-Actualization	_____	_____
		_____
		_____
5. Love	_____	_____
		_____
		_____
4. Esteem	_____	_____
		_____
		_____
3. Power and Control	_____	_____
		_____
		_____
2. Safety	_____	_____
		_____
		_____
1. Physiological	_____	_____
		_____
		_____

Know Thyself

Now you will condense the information you have been analyzing to identify your dominant style. In the first part we want you to look at the Personal Style you utilize when meeting your basic or more primal needs, this is your survival style. Typically, when one is motivated to meet these needs, the style is more intense and often comes automatically, without conscious thought.

Instructions: To recognize and reinforce your preferred style, consider the following and then complete the statements.

Look at the characters you listed when you indicated any of the first three motivators - Physiological, Safety, and Power and Control. Consider what they might all have in common. Identify a character that would best summarize all of them.

> When my <u>basic survival</u> needs (Physiological, Safety, or Power and Control) are the motivators, my Personal Style can be described as _____.
>   Character

The strengths in using this style are:

The difficulties in employing this style are:

Others may view this style as:

Now review the list of characters for the last five motivators - Esteem, Love, Self-Actualization, Manifested Actualization and Transcendence. These are indicative of your Personal Style when you are thriving. How would you best summarize these characters, your higher motivators?

> When my <u>higher needs</u> (Esteem, Love, Self-Actualization, Manifested Actualization or Transcendence) are the motivators, my Personal Style can be described as
> _____.
>   Character

The strengths in employing this style are:

The difficulties in employing this style are:

Others may view this style as:

Personal Style – Analysis and Reflection

Instructions: These are coaching questions, a means of reflecting on this exercise for greater insight. We recommend you review them and write down your thoughts.

1. How would you describe your Personal Style?

2. When is your Personal Style a great strength for you?

3. When is it a weaknesses or even a liability?

4. What Personal Style or characters would you see as being your exact opposite?

5. What differences did you notice in your Personal Style from childhood until now?

6. What patterns do you see in your characters and motivators? Do you have any ideas about why these patterns might exist?

Putting It All Together, *being*

The last exercise in this chapter is called "Putting It All Together," because it is your opportunity to pull together what you have learned, and coach yourself on your ***being***, or how you are in your life. Think of it like the story at the beginning of this chapter — you are completing your walkabout. You have come face-to-face with yourself, asking yourself questions, and experiencing the answers that are true for you.

In this chapter, you looked at your Life Interests, Character Traits and Personal Style. This is what we call your ***being***. Just as every person has different preferences in clothing or food, we all have ways of ***being*** that we have inherited, adopted or prefer. This is the ***being*** of the ***be, do, have*** paradigm discussed in the Introduction. The way we think about ***being*** is, first you must ***be*** something, then you ***do*** something, and ***having*** something is the result.

Part of this exercise involves recognizing the beliefs you hold around your Life Interests, Character Traits and Personal Style. Beliefs are the perceived truisms that define our view of the world. They can be helpful, guiding us as we travel life's journeys. But they can also limit and sabotage us, making us a victim and keeping us locked in status quo patterns. The key is to recognize your beliefs and challenge those that are not serving you.

You will also continue with the process you started in chapter 2, Life Purpose, by looking at the ***being*** portion of your purpose statement. Your purpose statement answers the question, "Why am I here and what should I do with my life?" What could you wrap your whole life around, such that when your time is up, you will feel fulfilled? One of the great joys in life is "living on purpose." It is what you give to future generations, and your contribution to the world.

Later, in chapters 4 and 5, you will continue with your Life Purpose, defining the ***doing*** and ***having*** portion, and then put it all together in a Life Purpose Statement.

As you continue to discover the different aspects of yourself, you will begin to realize how you can make them work for you. Although you may have predispositions through nature or nurture, the timing of when and where you utilize these aspects, as well as the potency with which you use them, is a choice.

Your Beliefs

So what are your beliefs around your Life Interests? Do you see your Life Interests as opening doors of opportunity, or do they limit you? What about your beliefs about your Character Traits and Personal Style? When we start to examine our beliefs, we see the prejudices about what we can and cannot have. Until we understand and recognize this, a silent but powerful dictator rules us.

An indication that you are on the right track as you answer the following questions is that you will *feel* something… passion, power, enlightenment, or maybe even rage or grief.

Instructions: In examining your beliefs regarding your Life Interests, Character Traits and Personal Style, we recommend that you do stream-of-consciousness writing. This means that you don't take a lot of time to ponder the statement, just start writing whatever thoughts come to your mind.

I believe that people with the kind of Life Interests, Character Traits and Personal Style I have work in jobs…

I believe that people with the Life Interests, Character Traits and Personal Style I have earn…

I believe that people with the Life Interests, Character Traits and Personal Style I have are…

I believe that people with the Life Interests, Character Traits and Personal Style I have live…

Instructions: Now take a closer look at your beliefs and answer the following questions. Note your attitude as you think about and write your answers.

Do each of your beliefs about your Life Interests, Character Traits and Personal Style empower or limit you? How?

Are your beliefs harmful to you or anyone else? How?

How might you address or alter your beliefs so that they support you to achieve *power, passion and joy*?

Life Purpose Statement

In chapter 2, you began to address the question of understanding your Life Purpose by answering some provocative and thought-provoking questions. You might want to take a moment to go back and read your answers and any comments you made on the Analysis and Reflection page at the end of that exercise, on page 25.

Now you will start the process of defining your purpose and creating a Life Purpose Statement, focusing first on the *being* aspect of the *be, do, have* paradigm. In subsequent chapters, you will address the *doing* and *having* themes.

Your Life Purpose Statement begins with understanding yourself. Start with the question, "Who am I and what are the Life Interests, Character Traits and Personal Style that constitute my *being*? This portion of the statement focuses on the person that you want to be as the foundation for your actions.

Instructions: List words or phrases in the spaces below that reflect the *being* themes about "the you" you have gotten to know. You are answering the question, *"What and who do you want to be in this world?"* Examples of *being* themes would be caring, spiritual, creative, teacher, influencer, curious, fun-loving, compassionate, etc.

_____   _____   _____

_____   _____   _____

_____   _____   _____

_____   _____   _____

Note any additional thoughts you have right now about your Life Purpose.

_____

_____

_____

_____

Putting It All Together, *being* – Analysis and Reflection

Instructions: These are coaching questions, a means of reflecting on this exercise for greater insight. We recommend you review them and write down your thoughts.

1. What are your observations about how you demonstrate who you are?

2. What did you learn about how you have been yourself and how you have not?

3. What insights did you gain about how you see yourself within the world?

4. What is the emerging theme about your life?

5. What changes would you like to make in how you present who you are? What things would you absolutely not change?

6. What could you do right now to move closer to living your life on purpose?

"Doing easily what others find difficult is talent; doing what is impossible for talent is genius."

—Henri Frederic Amiel

"Every man has his own vocation, talent is the call."

—Ralph Waldo Emerson

Success: Using Your Talents

What You Bring to the Job

We hope you are starting to see that all people bring "themselves" to their work. Beyond fulfilling a job description, you bring who you are, your style, aptitudes, skills, talents, beliefs and values: You are like no other person.

In this chapter, you will be working on identifying your Aptitudes and Skills. Through these exercises, you may discover skills you did not know you had, or rediscover ones you have not used in the context of your work. You will have the opportunity to explore what you are *doing*, what you want to be *doing*, and what others may want you to *do*.

In this chapter, you will start to gather information about your work experience. As we have mentioned, we refer to these exercises as Gathering Sheets.

In chapter 2, you identified your Life Interests and learned that your interests are based on what you love to *do* and desire; what comes *naturally* to you. Your aptitudes are usually thought of as what you were born with that *naturally* expresses itself. Skills describe what you are capable of *doing*. Skills are how you have chosen (or others did for you when you were young) to demonstrate your aptitudes. Your Life Interests can also influence the development of skills, supported by your aptitudes.

When Life Interests and Aptitudes and Skills combined with your needs or motivations, they create passion. Thus, the focus of this chapter is to shine a light on the combination that will enable conscious awareness and expression of this passion.

To recognize and appreciate your aptitudes and skills, you will be completing the following exercises:

- **Aptitudes and Skills**
  This exercise contains two parts. In the first part, you will identify your Aptitudes and Skills from a list. In the second part, you will refer to Your Stories and look for evidence of these talents.

- **Putting It All Together**
  This "Putting It All Together" exercise is focused on the ***doing*** aspect of the ***be, do, have*** paradigm. You will build on the activity started in chapter 3, looking at how your Aptitudes and Skills relate to your Life Purpose and Dream Work.

- **Gathering**
  You will use this first set of Gathering Sheets to record your experience. The objective is to collect all the materials that not only reinforce who you are, but are important to whom you want to become. This will help you respond to opportunities with substantiating information. It will also help you recognize all that you have experienced and accomplished.

Your Gathering activity will include your work as a company employee, or work you may have done while self-employed, as well as work performed in your home. This last area can be important for individuals who have been out of the workforce for some time. It can also be used to demonstrate Life Interests, Aptitudes and Skills, that are not reflected in your employment, or that you have not even recognized until now.

Aptitudes and Skills

Skills are developed. They are what we gain and improve by practice and knowledge, and what we use in the successful performance of our jobs. Skills that excite and motivate us to exercise them are often a good indicator of our natural gifts, or what we refer to as talents.

Skills are based on an aptitude, which is our natural ability. Think of an individual who has a natural aptitude for physical activities, coordination and dexterity, and with experience and practice turns that aptitude into a skill to play great soccer.

Understanding our aptitudes provides a platform for further development. "Dance with them that brung yuh" is an old country saying. It means that when you go with someone to a dance, you are first committed to dance with them, rather than looking for someone new.

This same principle applies to your Aptitudes and Skills. You are where you are and have had the successes that you've had because you already possess a set of Aptitudes and Skills that you depend on. These are the Aptitudes and Skills you have brought to the "dance." Your aptitudes, along with skills, provide a foundation as well as a compass to lead you to the next set of skills without having to "start all over again."

You can, however, refresh your motivation by reassessing your choices and reassembling the combination of your Life Interests and Aptitudes and Skills. In this exercise, you will start by examining who has "brung" you to the dance. Next, we encourage you to assess those combinations or the ones that tend to lead. And finally, you need to determine which combination you desire to lead you now. Will you be led by adding more of your interests, or reinterpreting the use of your aptitudes? Or maybe will you choose to develop a new skill that encourages the expression of your talent?

Aptitudes and Skills - Part A

Instructions: Take a look at the list of Aptitudes and Skills below. This list, while not all-inclusive, allows you to explore your aptitudes and how you have used them in the skills you have developed. It can be helpful to think of an aptitude and skill as a pair; if you didn't have that aptitude, you would never have developed that skill. *A skill is an aptitude that is realized.* For example, you may have an aptitude of an athlete with a developed skill in playing basketball but not golf. Or you may have an analytical aptitude expressed as a skill in research but not financial planning. Aptitudes are typically expressed as adjectives, what you are *being*, and skills as verbs, or what you *do*.

Start by going through the list of Aptitudes and circle the words that apply to you. Feel free to add to the list in the spaces at the bottom.

Aptitudes

Analytical	Creative	Independent	Imaginative
Artistic	Visionary	Manipulative	Visionary
Cautious	Deductive	Detail oriented	Persuasive
Organized	Discerning	Communication	Methodical
Leadership	Humorous	Memorization	Dexterity
Mechanical	Empathetic	Problem solving	Verbal
Ambitious	Self motivated	Accuracy	Mathematical
Intellectual	Organized	Flexible	Expressionistic
Inquisitive	Philosophical	Athletic	Spatial

Innovative	Rational	Strategic	Precision
Competitive	Adaptable	Process oriented	Visual
Logical	Learner	Coordinated	Musical
Systematic	Argumentative	Initiative	Observant
Insightful	Scientific	Loyal	Numerical
Conceptual	Social	Commonsense	Reasoning
Entrepreneurial	Conciliatory	Confidence	

Now go through the list of Skills and circle the words that apply to you. Again, you can add to the list in the spaces at the bottom.

Skills:

Clerical	Articulate	Organizing	Budgeting
Mechanic	Music	Selling	Networking
Sports	Managing	System thinking	Memorizing
Leading	Counseling	Composing	Promotion
Interpersonal	Drawing	Constructing	Research
Factual	Painting	Interpersonal	Writing
Political	Designing	Decision making	Orchestrating
Mathematics	Persuading	Reading	Supervising
Administration	Comic	Negotiation	Building
Teaching	Empowering	Planning	Calculations
Team work	Manipulating	Engineering	Inspirational
Technology	Motivating	Speaking	Counseling

Aptitudes and Skills - Part B

Instructions: Review Your Stories and identify the specific Aptitudes and Skills that you demonstrated. If, in looking at the story it is not clear which Aptitudes and Skills might have come into play, think of how you would describe the person in the story in terms of their abilities. What ability enabled them to do what it is they did? What skills do you have a particular gift for that you demonstrate time and time again? Do you tend to use a particular aptitude over and over in a variety of ways?

Here is an example from Mary's story about the girl and the playground. Found on page 15.

5 to 10 years of age

The aptitudes are: *Initiation, as demonstrated in choosing to get involved, compassion, as demonstrated by caring for another person, community involvement, demonstrated in the thought that everyone is equally important, curiosity, demonstrated in thinking about what the girl's story might be, and altruism in not focusing on the possible consequences to myself.*

The skills are: *Initiating activities, such as standing with the girl, Innovating something new when it is not commonly accepted by others, such as standing with the girl instead of going with the group, Investigating outside of what I already knew, to see what else was there, Interpersonal, in relating with others such as the girl, and Utilizing my Power to make a difference for someone else and myself, as opposed to her telling me to get lost.*

Birth to 5 years of age

The aptitudes are: _____

The skills are: _____

5 to 10 years of age

The aptitudes are: _____

The skills are: _____

10 to 15 years of age

The aptitudes are: _____

The skills are: _____

15 to 20 years of age

The aptitudes are: _____

The skills are: _____

20 to 25 years of age

The aptitudes are: _____

The skills are: _____

25 to 30 years of age

The aptitudes are: _____

The skills are: _____

30 to 35 years of age

The aptitudes are: _____

The skills are: _____

35 to 40 years of age

The aptitudes are: _____

The skills are: _____

40 to 45 years of age

The aptitudes are: _____

The skills are: _____

45 to 50 years of age

The aptitudes are: _____

The skills are: _____

50 to 55 years of age

The aptitudes are: _____

The skills are: _____

55 to 60 years of age

The aptitudes are: _____

The skills are: _____

60 to 65 years of age

The aptitudes are: _____

The skills are: _____

65 to 70 years of age

The aptitudes are: _____

The skills are: _____

70 to 75 years of age

The aptitudes are: _____

The skills are: _____

75 to 80 years of age

The aptitudes are: _____

The skills are: _____

80 plus years of age

The aptitudes are: _____

The skills are: _____

Aptitudes and Skills – Analysis and Reflection

Instructions: These are coaching questions, a means of reflecting on this exercise for greater insight. We recommend you review them and write down your thoughts.

1. How would you describe your talents overall?

2. How are you utilizing your talents to motivate and inspire you?

3. What additional skills would you like to develop?

4. What Aptitudes and Skills are you using in your current position?

5. What Aptitudes and Skills do you feel you cannot utilize in your current position?

6. What changes would you make in your current position to greater utilize your talents?

Putting It All Together, *doing*

Are our talents really the call to our vocation, as the quote at the beginning of the chapter states? What makes some people excel, dare to go where only the brave dare to go, and reach that unreachable star? What makes some people know what they want to **do** when they grow up? How do you begin to know what you are supposed to be ***doing***? If you are good at something, does it mean that you must use that talent even if you do not want to?

The answers to these questions are dependent on what it is you need and want at this point in your life. We refer to this as the work hierarchy.

If you are motivated by physiological needs, such as getting money to put a roof over your head and food on your table, then you probably really want and need a job. If you lack any real work experience in the world because you are young, you may need to take several jobs to gain experience from which to draw. A job is where you can develop new skills and hone those that come naturally, giving your aptitudes and interests a playing field to know them better. You experience and breathe life into your aptitudes (also referred to as strengths) by practicing them in some way.

If you want more than a job, you are ready to express your power and passion and how you fit into the world of work; you are looking for a career. If you are choosing a career, or are in one already, you can ask yourself whether what you are choosing is in alignment with who you are, what you want to **do**, and what motivates you.

If you have had jobs or experienced a career, and are looking for more, you are being drawn to a vocation. A vocation is something you are called to **do**, coupled with your life experiences. Our talents can be a call to our vocation. Your choices are not just based on what you are suited for, but what gets you fired up and propels you forward. In a vocation you are motivated beyond physical, safety, and belonging needs, or even self-esteem reinforcements such as money, relationships, or accolades. You get joy in the contributions you are making to the world. Because what you are ***doing*** is a joy and pleasure for you, it sustains itself and gives you more joy in the experience of you ***being*** the one ***doing*** it.

So whether your goal is a job, a career or a vocation, the secret is to understand your needs, interests, traits and style. In chapter 3, you gathered information on aspects of your ***being***. In this chapter, you have examined your Aptitudes and Skills, or what your preferences for *what* you ***do***. Now let's combine what you desire to ***do*** with who you are, or are ***being***.

Your Beliefs

Remember, beliefs are personal truisms, what we do not tend to question that defines our view of the world. In the last chapter, "Know Thyself," you addressed your beliefs about your Life Interests, Character Traits and Personal Style. Was this difficult? Did you find that your beliefs in that chapter might be sabotaging who you want to be, perhaps limiting any expression of expertise, let alone talent? Look further into your beliefs regarding your Aptitudes and Skills to see if you may be placing unnecessary restrictions on yourself, or not giving yourself the help you need to develop those "diamonds in the rough" that you possess.

Instructions: In looking at your beliefs regarding your Aptitudes and Skills, we recommend that you do stream-of-consciousness writing. This means you don't take a lot of time to ponder the statement, but just start writing whatever thoughts come to your mind.

I believe that people with the kind of Aptitudes and Skills I have work in jobs …

I believe that people with the Aptitudes and Skills I have earn …

I believe that people with the Aptitudes and Skills I have are …

I believe that people with the Aptitudes and Skills I have live …

Instructions: As you did in the last chapter, take a look at what you have written about your beliefs and answer the following questions.

Do each of your beliefs about your Aptitudes and Skills empower or limit you? How?

Are your beliefs harmful to you or anyone else? How?

How might you address or alter your beliefs so that they support you to achieve power, passion and joy?

Life Purpose Statement

This is the next step in defining your Life Purpose and creating a Life Purpose Statement. In chapter 2, you answered a number of questions to reflect on what is important to you. In chapter 3, you started to define your Life Purpose by looking at your ***being***. You are now going to look at the ***doing*** portion of your Life Purpose.

Throughout this chapter, you have recognized your aptitudes and identified the skills you possess. You have looked at some of the beliefs that have developed. Ask yourself, "What Aptitudes and Skills align with the person I choose to ***be***; what do I really want to be ***doing*** with my time?"

Don't hesitate to look back to your previous work in chapters 2 and 3 or to review the *be, do, have* paradigm in the Introduction.

Instructions: In the space below, list words or phrases that reflect the ***doing*** themes about "the you" that you have gotten to know. This is about what you ***do***. You are answering the question, "What do I want to ***do***, or continue to ***do***, in this world?" Examples of ***doing*** themes would be writing, researching, managing, organizing, jumping, lifting, measuring, singing, playing, etc.

_____   _____   _____

_____   _____   _____

_____   _____   _____

_____   _____   _____

Now write down any ideas you have so far regarding your Life Purpose. If you were to **do** these things, who might you **be**, and what might be the results of your choices? You will continue to build upon these ideas to write your actual Life Purpose Statement in chapter 6.

_____

_____

_____

_____

_____

Putting It All Together, *doing* – Analysis and Reflection

Instructions: These are coaching questions, a means of reflecting on this exercise for greater insight. We recommend you review them and write down your thoughts.

1. "My Aptitudes and Skills are expressed through my actions and impact what I have come to believe about life." In what ways is this statement true for you?

2. What observations can you make about how you demonstrate who you are?

3. What insights did you gain about your skill level and talents?

4. What aptitudes could you develop further, into perhaps different skills than you have previously exercised?

5. Do you see a theme emerging? What conclusion, if any, can you presently make about your situation?

6. What changes would you like to make in the expression of your aptitudes, the development of your skills and the use of your talents?

Gathering – Employment History

What follows is the first of your "gathering sheets." As we discussed in the Introduction, Gathering Sheets are the placeholders for the Living Portfolio you are compiling through this process. Pay attention to the Aptitudes and Skills and evidence of talent as you complete this work, in case you might have missed something in "Your Stories."

In this section you will collect the following information:

- **Employment**
  This is a listing of all the jobs you have ever held, along with the relevant information. No job is unimportant, and it may provide important clues as to what you may be up to *doing* next, as well as who you were **being** at that time. Document all that you remember regarding responsibilities and tasks. This is often more important than the job title or where you performed the work.

- **Self-Employment**
  You will create a list of all the work you have performed while self-employed. Entrepreneurial ventures are not always successful in the long run, but as we say, "there are no failures." Even if you do not consider your venture a long-term success, include it. Be sure to describe not only the nature of your business, but also all the personal responsibilities and tasks you performed.

- **Work In the Home**
  You will create a list of all the responsibilities and tasks you have performed working in your home. This is about recognizing all the aptitudes, skills, interests and talents that you used. It is critical when you have been a stay-at-home parent, spouse or student, or experience concentrated time at home for any reason, to recognize and translate into business skills all the work you performed in that role. For instance, if you were responsible for balancing the checkbook, verifying charges and watching the budget, you have demonstrated the ability to plan, manage and document expenses. While you may not be interested in this type of work, it can demonstrate your ability to organize, plan and manage.

Employment

Instructions: Begin organizing your thoughts and information here. Include the following information:

- ⇨ Employer, with address
- ⇨ Dates of employment
- ⇨ Positions held
- ⇨ Descriptions of responsibilities

Employer _____ Dates _____

    Address _____

Position _____

Responsibilities _____

Employer _____ Dates _____

    Address _____

Position _____

Responsibilities _____

Employer _____ Dates _____

    Address _____

Position _____

Responsibilities _____

Self-Employment

Instructions: Begin organizing your thoughts and information here. Include the following information:

- ➪ Name or type of business
- ➪ Description
- ➪ Dates of operation
- ➪ Roles and responsibilities

Name or Type _____ Dates _____

_____

Description _____

Roles and Responsibilities _____

Name or Type _____ Dates _____

_____

Description _____

Roles and Responsibilities _____

Name or Type _____ Dates _____

_____

Description _____

Roles and Responsibilities _____

Work In the Home

Instructions: Begin organizing your thoughts and information here. Include the following information:

⇨ Role performed
⇨ Tasks or responsibilities
⇨ Skills required

Role
_____

Tasks/responsibilities
_____
_____

Skills
_____

Role
_____

Tasks/responsibilities
_____
_____

Skills
_____

Role
_____

Tasks/responsibilities
_____
_____

Skills
_____

Gathering – Analysis and Reflection

Instructions: These are coaching questions, a means of reflecting on this exercise for greater insight. We recommend that you review them and write down your thoughts.

1. What did you observe about your employment history?

2. What positions and/or employers are your most memorable? Why?

3. What work have you done outside a specific job that you are proud of?

4. If you were an entrepreneur, what would you do?

5. What do you enjoy doing the most around your home?

6. What work have you done that you dislike?

"When love and skill work together, expect a masterpiece."

— John Ruskin

"Serendipity, look for something, find something else, and realize that what you've found is more suited to your needs than what you thought you were looking for."

—Lawrence Block

The Right Fit 5

What Will Work for You?

This chapter will help you recognize your values and the work culture and environment that are right for you.

Did you ever feel your personal values were in conflict with those of your employer and others in your workplace? In what kinds of work environments do you thrive? What types of people make you feel comfortable? What books do you read, what movies do you watch, and in what kinds of activities do you participate?

Your answers provide clues to the environment that is best for you. For example, if you are easygoing in nature, like the great outdoors, prefer solitude, and are active in Green Peace, a Fortune 500 company in a high-rise building located in a metropolitan area may provide a nice contrast, but would more likely be a huge disaster. If you prefer entrepreneurial work and are in a job that is highly structured with rules and procedures, it may cause you to believe you are inadequate, and worse, your peers and supervisors could feel that way too.

By completing the following exercises of discovery, you will identify your current relationship with your values and work preferences.

- **True Values**
  In the True Values exercises, you will identify both your intrinsic or internal values, and your extrinsic or external values. Narrowing your choices down to your top seven will give you the opportunity to begin to see possible value conflicts, either with your internal values, or how these values translate to your job and your workplace.

- **Preferred Employer**
  This exercise will help you identify how well your philosophical system matches the philosophical system of your employer, and where you might make trade-offs.

- **Work Environment**
  Work Environment refers to both the physical and psychological aspects of where you work. You will analyze how you feel about the elements of your Work Environment, including the preferred leadership and work styles of your managers, supervisors and co-workers, as well as the physical environment of the workplace.

- **Putting It All Together**
  This last Putting It All Together exercise will focus on the *have* of the *be, do, have* paradigm. You will have the opportunity to summarize your discoveries around your True Values, Preferred Employer and Work Environment issues, identify your beliefs about these aspects of work, and pull together your purpose statements into one succinct statement.

True Values

We cannot begin to understand what we want from work without a thorough examination of our values. The True Values exercise you are about to do is an important step in recognizing what kind of work environments you enjoy and will best support you.

The dictionary defines a value as "a principle, standard, or quality considered worthwhile or desirable." To some, values determine what is right and what is wrong. Values shape and guide the way we live our lives and affect all the decisions we make. Often, our actions speak louder than words about what we really value.

For you to feel comfortable with your employer and your colleagues, there must be a reasonable match with your values. If there are major conflicts, something must give. Either you must be willing to make trade-offs, or you will have to seek an employer with a better value fit. It is not a matter of either being right or wrong; it's whether you are in alignment in your workplace with what is important to you.

Like filters, True Values are indicative of how you measure the world, and they direct your motivation. True Values don't often change, but you can hold particular values more strongly when they are motivated by a particular need. Values also affect all the decisions we make, whether business decisions, a choice of religion, a chosen career path, or even parental or educational beliefs. Values are essential to who we are. True Values are foundational to personal motivation, and how we meet our needs.

To help you recognize your True Values we will divide them into internal values and external values. The internal values that direct you affect what evidence you look for in choosing and being satisfied with your workplace. Your internal values are met when they match an external value or the physical evidence of that value. True Value match is the key to joy in any environment.

This exercise consists of four parts. In Part A, you will identify your internal values, what many call your internal compass, and then in Part B, you will look for evidence of these values in Your Stories. In Part C, you will translate your internal values into what you want from your work. How do your internal values get expressed in your workplace in the form of external values? In Part D, you will narrow your choices down to seven internal values and seven external values, verifying that they are *True* Values.

True Values – Part A

In this first step begin by examining your internal values.

Instructions: Begin by becoming familiar with the internal values listed below. Read through the list and circle the words that you believe best describe your values. This is not a complete list, so feel free to add values at the bottom.

Values – Internal

Honesty	Flexibility	Creativity	Risk taking
Humor	Aesthetics	Equality	Education
Compassion	Logic	Luxury	Independence
Justice	Reason	Sensuality	Humility
Innovation	Integrity	Excitement	Pride

Spontaneity	Love	Persistence	Spirituality
Entertainment	Self-worth	Perseverance	Nurturing
Ambition	Independence	Adventure	Self-sacrifice
Order	Self-confidence	Dependability	Art
Caution	Respect	Physical expression	Change
Dependability	Interdependence	Physical activity	Stability
Loyalty	Imagination	Mental activity	Solitude
Friendship	Fun	Gentility	Money
Courage	Patriotism	Cooperation	Teaching
Generosity	Relaxation	Law	Attention
Conservation	Knowledge	Nature	Diversity
Dialogue	Privacy	Competition	Time
Synthesis	Strength	Curiosity	Freedom
Relationship	Passion	Cooperation	Stress
Responsibility	Control	Peace	Simplicity
Family	Power	Choice	Choice
Stress	Simplicity	Harmony	
_____	_____	_____	_____
_____	_____	_____	_____

The Right Fit

True Values – Part B

Instructions: Go back to "Your Stories" in chapter 2, pages 16-18. With the values list as a guide, identify which internal values appear to be reflected in each of Your Stories. Which internal values motivated your actions or inactions?

Here is an example from Bob's story of the young marine, on page 15.

15 to 20 years of age

My internal values in this story were: *justice, flexibility, integrity, caution, loyalty, courage, responsibility, patriotism, persistence, dependability, spirituality and freedom.*

Birth to 5 years of age

My internal values in this story were: _____

5 to 10 years of age

My internal values in this story were: _____

10 to 15 years of age

My internal values in this story were: _____

15 to 20 years of age

My internal values in this story were: _____

20 to 25 years of age

My internal values in this story were: _____

25 to 30 years of age

My internal values in this story were: _____

30 to 35 years of age

My internal values in this story were: _____

35 to 40 years of age

My internal values in this story were: _____
_____

40 to 45 years of age

My internal values in this story were: _____
_____

45 to 50 years of age

My internal values in this story were: _____
_____

50 to 55 years of age

My internal values in this story were: _____
_____

55 to 60 years of age

My internal values in this story were: _____
_____

60 to 65 years of age

My internal values in this story were: _____
_____

65 to 70 years of age

My internal values in this story were: _____
_____

70 to 75 years of age

My internal values in this story were: _____
_____

75 to 80 years of age

My internal values in this story were: _____
_____

80 plus years of age

My internal values in this story were: _____
_____

True Values – Part C

Next take a look at your external values. Although we are not asking you to specifically analyze Your Stories in this part of the True Values exercise, think about the values present in Your Stories. This evidence of internal values most likely held the seed of an external value that perhaps is still important to you.

Instructions: Review the list of external values and circle the words that represent how your internal values would show up in the workplace. As an example, if one of your internal values is integrity, would you want a work environment that demonstrates honesty in its dealings with customers, or colleagues who are honest or have a sense of safety while at work? This is not a complete list, so feel free to add values at the bottom.

Values – External

Job stability	Accountability	Pleasant surroundings	Competition
Unstructured	Business standards	Location	Stimulation
Structured	Ethical	Key position	Effective
Benefits	Responsibilities	Autonomy	Efficiency
Leadership	Mobility	Flexible schedule	Physical work
Artistic expression	Job flexibility	Ecologically friendly	Independence
Expertise	Security	Sense of community	Cooperation
High compensation	Creativity	Friendships	Fun
Job diversity	Authority	Safety	Rewards
Decision making	Learning opportunities	Continued employment	Recognition
Friendly environment	Problem-solving	Travel	Growth
Proximity to work	Safe environment	Educational opportunities	Stress free
Training others	Fast-paced	Challenges	Exercising Intellect
_____	_____	_____	_____
_____	_____	_____	_____

True Values – Part D

Now let's look at the values you identified, internal and external, and "road test" them to verify that these are your "True" Values. A True Value is a value that is genuine when the answers to the following three questions are positive:

- Did you select this value as an ideal value in which you absolutely believe?
- Would you protect and defend this value under any and all circumstances?
- Are your actions on this value consistent and compatible with the value itself?

Instructions: Look at the internal values you circled in Part A or identified in Your Stories in Part B, and the external values you circled in Part C. Ask the three questions about each of them. Answering "no" to any of the questions does not mean that a particular value is unimportant to you. Just be clear about which values truly drive you and what you are not willing to compromise on or ignore. Create a list of the values that are your True Values.

True Values — Internal	True Values — External

Instructions: Chances are, you identified a large number of internal and external values. We are now going to force you to identify the seven of each group of values with the highest priority because it is hard to focus on more than this. The general rule is seven, plus or minus two, as the maximum amount of items that we can actively manage. Even if in narrowing them down you leave a number of True Values behind, know that they are still influencing you and your choices. Which values are you not willing to live without? Which values would you most want people to associate with you? Don't fight this — we are requiring you to make some trade-offs so you will think about which values are really important to you.

My top seven internal values and how I would express in external values are:

Internal Values

1.
2.
3.
4.
5.
6.
7.

External Values

1.
2.
3.
4.
5.
6.
7.

True Values – Analysis and Reflection

Instructions: These are coaching questions, a means of reflecting on this exercise for greater insight. We recommend you review them and write down your thoughts.

1. What insights did you gain about your True Values and how they relate to your career?

2. Were there any True Values identified that seem to conflict or contradict one another? If so, explain. What may be your trade-offs?

3. What True Values did you find are in complete agreement with your employer and the employees in the organization?

4. What True Values did you find are in conflict with those of your employer and the employees in the organization? Rate these conflicts as high, medium, or low.

5. What conclusion can you make about your True Values and your work?

6. What change could you make right now to gain greater alignment with your True Values?

Preferred Employer

Another aspect of finding joy in work is to understand what types of employers and environments support us to be successful. As a member of an organization, it is important to recognize, understand, and be in alignment with its culture. This means having an understanding of the philosophy of an employer and how well it fits with your personal philosophy. It means being comfortable with the style of the employer, the work process, and how you are rewarded. *If we are not in alignment, then a great deal of our energy may be directed toward unproductive activity.*

There are two parts to the Preferred Employer exercise. In Part A, you will describe your ideal organization by looking at four aspects. The following four aspects constitute the philosophy system, or culture of an organization. In Part B, you will examine how you align in these areas with your current or most recent employer.

- **Expectations** are what you want from an employer and its leaders, and what an employer and its leaders want from you. They include rules and regulations, dress code, etc. Remember that there are both formal and informal expectations.

- **Value System** are the principles of an employer, or what it stands for. The value system includes the vision, mission, character, integrity, policies, etc. of the employer.

- **Rewards and Recognition** refers to the salary system of the organization, and includes bonus qualifications, benefits, and special compensation through gifts. It also takes into account other types of recognition, including special acknowledgement and treatment.

- **Objectives** indicate why an organization exists. What purpose does it serve in the world, and what is its direction?

You may not have given much thought to some of these areas. One approach is to look at the organizations where you are currently or most recently employed, and think about what you liked about them and why you worked there. Then look at what you didn't like about the organization, and why you wanted to, or did leave. (The Gathering Sheets you completed in chapter 4 listing all your work experiences will help.) The goal is to have you assess the things you can and cannot live with, how you can leverage those things that are positive, and what, if anything, you can do about any incongruence you identify.

Preferred Employer – Part A

Instructions: Answer the following questions to identify the characteristics of your ideal environment.

1. Expectations
What are your expectations of an employer?

What do you believe an employer should expect from you?

What are some examples of expectations with which you have been in conflict?

2. Value System
Which employer values or principles are important to you?

Based on the work you did in True Values, page 82, how would you describe your personal value system?

What are some examples of employer values with which you have been in conflict?

3. Rewards and Recognition
How should an employer reward and recognize an employee?

How should exceeding expectations be recognized?

How should you earn a bonus or other recognition?

What types of rewards and recognition motivate you?

4. Objectives
What employer goals and objectives can you relate to?

What types of employer objectives do not coincide with your values?

What are your personal objectives?

Preferred Employer – Part B

Now let's look at your current work situation.

Instructions: Compare your current or most recent employment with the results of your analysis in Part A. Do you find alignment or gaps?

1. Expectations
I would describe the expectations of my current organization as:

I am in alignment with:

I am *not* in alignment with:

2. Value System
I would describe the values of my current organization as:

I am in alignment with:

I am *not* in alignment with:

3. Rewards and Recognition
I would describe the reward and recognition system of my current organization as:

I am in alignment with:

I am *not* in alignment with:

4. Objectives
I would describe the objectives of my current organization as:

I am in alignment with:

I am *not* in alignment with:

Instructions: Consider the following questions:

What conclusions do you have regarding your Preferred Employer philosophy system?

How well do you fit into the system and processes where you are currently employed?

Preferred Employer – Analysis and Reflection

Instructions: These are coaching questions, a means of reflecting on this exercise for greater insight. We recommend you review them and write down your thoughts.

1. Which of the four aspects of an employer's philosophy system (Expectations, Value System, Rewards and Recognition, and Objectives) had the most impact?

2. Which of these areas will bring you the greatest happiness or joy at work?

3. Which of the four areas is working for you with your current employer?

4. Which of the four areas is not working for you and how would you want it to change? What is your greatest challenge?

5. What type of employer do you believe would be the best match for you? Explain.

6. What changes do you think you can realistically make in your current situation?

Work Environment

We are now going to take a look at some of the specific aspects of an organization's Work Environment. Beyond the mission and values of an organization, what is the actual environment like — from the style of leadership, to the work style, to the type of people who are drawn to and work in the organization, to the actual physical space? This is about the comfort you feel when you are at work.

We once coached an employee who went from a great performance to a mediocre one. He was doing the same job, but after he moved to a new location, he had not performed to his usual standard. After much conversation, we figured out that he had a problem with working in the high-rise building where he was now located. In the few months since he had moved, he had been experiencing dizzy spells that ultimately were diagnosed as an inner ear problem. He could actually feel the building sway and was "sea sick" most of the time. He was moved to a lower floor, and his performance returned to the high level it had been. This may seem like an extreme example of the impact of physical space, but it is not that unusual. Take a look at all four of the aspects we call Work Environment to determine what is important to you.

- **Leadership**

    What style of leadership do you work best under? Have you thought about the best jobs you have held and the style your direct leader or the leadership team possessed? There are certain leadership behaviors that are an asset to performance and morale: fair treatment, respect, honesty, integrity and competency, to name just a few. Style of personal leadership will also impact our interactions, communications and involvement with leaders.

- **Work Style**

    Work style refers to the way in which individuals in your current organization get work done. Do you work in a fast-paced environment where everyone works long hours and at warp speed? Or is the Work Environment laid-back, with actual work time limited, and a lot of time spent socializing or doing non-work activities? Is your personal life valued and respected?

    We often learn to adjust and conform to the style of the organization, but at what cost? If you are an ambitious, hard-driving individual who is in an organization that has a laid-back work style, you may find yourself having difficulty with your colleagues. In another scenario, you might be at a point in your life where having time for your family may not coincide with a Work Environment which demands complete commitment. In some cases the differences may not be so extreme, but it is beneficial to know what your style is at this point in your life, and whether you are conforming.

- **People**

    The people we work with play a big role in how we feel about our job. Whether you are an extremely social individual who values and needs contact with other individuals, or you prefer to work alone, the reality is that we work in organizations with other people. Consider the best work relationships for you. Do you want colleagues who you can socialize with after work, who share common interests or are at the same phase in their lives as you are? Or would you prefer to work in a highly structured organization with a focus on credentials and college degrees? Is the commitment of your colleagues important, or just your relationships?

    How important is teamwork, and how would you describe it? In most organizations today, teamwork is critical to getting the job done. Do you know how to be a good team member?

How do you feel about the issues of diversity? Does the fact that your colleagues represent a variety of backgrounds and races excite you, or do you resent or feel uncomfortable with a focus on diversity?

- **Physical Environment**
  Your physical environment includes the building you work in, the location, the space you are provided, the equipment you have to get work done, and the supplies. The reality is that for some people, their physical surroundings are crucial to their overall mood and sense of well-being. For others, it is less important.

Instructions: Answer the questions in each section, being as detailed as possible in your description.

1. Leadership
Describe your favorite leader.

You worked the best with that leader because:

Describe your worst leader.

As a leader, you are, or will in the future be described as:

2. Work Style
I feel the current work style of my organization is:

In my most successful work experience, I would describe that work style as:

Because of my life situation and priorities, my current work style is:

The worst work style I have experienced was:

What I would change about the current work style in my organization is:

3. People
I would describe my colleagues as:

What is missing from my current work environment relative to my colleagues is:

What I would miss about my colleagues, if I were to leave, would be:

My ideal situation with colleagues is:

4. Physical Environment

What I like best about my physical environment is:

The worst part of my physical surroundings is:

If I were to compare my home to my office, I would describe the difference as:

My ideal job would be located:

The physical environment I feel most happy and productive in is:

Work Environment – Analysis and Reflection

Instructions: These are coaching questions, a means of reflecting on this exercise for greater insight. We recommend you review them and write down your thoughts.

1. What did you discover about yourself relative to your current leadership?

2. What did you discover about the impact your colleagues have on your work satisfaction?

3. What did you discover about the impact of work style on your performance

4. What did you discover about the impact of your physical surroundings?

5. Look at your responses to the previous four questions. How would you describe your ideal Work Environment?

6. What changes could you personally make that would make your Work Environment more compatible?

Putting It All Together, *having*

Remember the quote on serendipity at the beginning of this chapter? It's now time to see if you have experienced any *serendipity* while going through the exercises in this chapter. Did you expect to identify something you believed about yourself but realized something else instead? Was it a surprise?

You have completed exercises for True Values, Preferred Employer and Work Environment. Some things you learned, or confirmed about your preferences in these three areas, may have come as an enlightening revelation to you. It is important to understand which of your preferences in the three areas are absolutes and which are trade-offs. The absolutes are values and preferences that are "a must" for you to experience joy in your work. The trade-offs are values and preferences you are willing to delay having right away, things you are willing to live without because of other priorities, until you can satisfy them in other ways, or eventually make them part of your career environment.

The questions in Putting It All Together will help you confirm what you have learned from this chapter's exercises, and will help you verify your absolutes and trade-offs. You will also work on the final aspect of your Life Purpose.

Your Beliefs

Remember that beliefs are the truisms that define our view of the world. In the last chapter's section on "Putting It All Together," you addressed your beliefs about your skills and abilities. Was this difficult? Did you find that your beliefs might be sabotaging your true abilities or talents?

Instructions: In looking at your beliefs regarding your True Values, Preferred Employer and Work Environment, we recommend that you do stream-of-conscious writing. This means that you don't take a lot of time to ponder the statement, but just start writing whatever thoughts come to your mind.

I believe that people with the kinds of True Values, Preferred Employer and Work Environment preferences I have work in jobs…

I believe that people with the True Values, Preferred Employer and Work Environment preferences I have earn…

I believe that people with the True Values, Preferred Employer and Work Environment preferences I have live…

I believe that people with the True Values, Preferred Employer and Work Environment preferences I have are…

Instructions: As you did in the last chapter, take a look at what you have written about your beliefs and answer the following questions.

Do each of your beliefs about your True Values, Preferred Employer and Work Environment *empower* or *limit* you? How?

Are your beliefs harmful to you or anyone else? How?

How might you address or alter your beliefs so that they support you to achieve *power, passion and joy*?

Life Purpose Statement

This is your third exercise addressing the question of finding your Life Purpose. You may again want to go back and review your previous work. Now you are going to write about what you would like based on who you are. This is the portion of your Life Purpose statement that addresses manifestation, or *having*.

In Putting It All Together for this chapter, you have recognized the True Values you hold most dear, the preferences you have for a Preferred Employer, and what Work Environments support you. You have accomplished a great deal regarding the *being* and *doing* portion of the equation. Now, in looking at the *having*, or the results, you have the opportunity to identify the "fruits of your labor."

Start by listing words or phrases in the space below that reflect the *having* themes about "the you" you have gotten to know. You will be answering the question, "What do you want to *have* from this world?" Examples of *having* themes can be flexibility, love, awareness, appreciation, profitability, teamwork, community, enlightenment, education, success, rewards, recognition, etc.

_____   _____   _____

_____   _____   _____

_____   _____   _____

_____   _____   _____

Now you have the opportunity to write down any additional thoughts you have regarding a Life Purpose Statement. If you were to *do* what you do, *being* who you are, what would you likely then *have*?

_____

_____

_____

_____

Putting It All Together, *having* – Analysis and Reflection

Instructions: These are coaching questions, a means of reflecting on this exercise for great insight. We recommend you review them and write down your thoughts.

1. My True Values impact my preferences for a Preferred Employer and Work Environment, which results in what I *have*. What patterns do you see relative to this statement in your work life?

2. What did you learn about your beliefs regarding your True Values, Preferred Employer and Work Environment?

3. Do any of your beliefs feel negative or like a judgment?

4. Do you see a potential conflict between the *being, doing* or *having* portion of your Life Purpose Statement? What is it?

5. How does your current employer and your environment support what you would like to *have*?

6. How do you feel about all the work you have done thus far?

"Success is the progressive realization of a worthwhile dream."

— Dexter Yager

"Don't be afraid to give your best to what seemingly are small jobs. Every time you conquer one, it makes you that much stronger. If you do the little jobs well, the big ones tend to take care of themselves."

— Dale Carnegie

Getting Where You Are Going

Setting Your Course

Do you remember the first Key Message from the introduction?

"If you don't care where you're going, it doesn't matter which way you go."

This chapter is about defining the goals that set a direction for your life and what you **do**. Your work goals should focus on the professional and personal achievements, skills and knowledge you want to acquire over the next several years. Once established, your goals will bring clarity in establishing a personal development strategy and long-term career plan. It will help you cope with uneasiness about where you are and what you might really want to **do**.

"If you don't believe anything will change, it won't. And if you never give anything a try, it can't."

— Prudence

Have you heard the story about the man caught in a flood who was praying to be rescued from his situation? He kept praying for God to save him. When people came to help him wade out, he refused and said, "God will save me." When a rowboat came as the water was rising, he refused to get in and said, "God will save me." When the water had reached the roof and a helicopter flew over, he waved it off and said, "God will save me." Later, when he met God in heaven, he asked, "Why didn't you save me?" God responded, "I sent rescuers, a row boat and a helicopter. Why didn't you get in?" The moral of the story is, even if you are waiting for life to bring solutions for what you desire and hope for, you still have to be watching and willing to try what comes your way. And sometimes the answer just doesn't look the way we think it will, or it will take longer than we like or are comfortable with.

Goals involve the ability to read the synchronicity, timing and meaning in relation to the actions and results that occur. Given this perspective, goals are very valuable as a backdrop to what happens, and also what doesn't. By looking at goals from this point of view, you will begin to discern whether or not achieving your stated goal is really what you desire, or maybe you just thought it was or *should* be. Results and expectations can truly test your commitment! You will start to see many goals surfacing naturally through the action of compiling this portfolio, and possibly see others diminish. Now is the time to make clear statements of what you truly intend to accomplish and how you plan to make it happen. Then if change occurs in your desire or ability to meet these goals, it will allow other choices to be deliberate and not occur below your radar or masquerade as no choice at all.

Goals should be viewed as guiding principles that *you* are in charge of, not vice versa. To clarify your goals, you will be completing the following exercises:

- **Roles and Goals**
  This exercise will help you determine if there are issues between your Roles and Goals, goals and goals, or roles and roles. It will help you discover the conflicts and decide what to do about them.

- **Finding Your Joy**
  This will be your opportunity to define what you truly want. You will build on the work you have done in previous chapters on your Life Purpose Statement and then create your Dream Work reflecting who you would **be**, what you would choose to **do** and what you want to **have**.

Roles and Goals

We believe that goal setting work must be done in combination with the roles we play. Our goals are what we want out of life, and our roles are what we are willing to do to attain them. To do this exercise, you will need to go back and review the work you completed in Life Facets in chapter 2.

As you begin this exercise, we want you to focus on the following two realities of work life management:

There is an inevitable relationship in life between roles and goals. It is difficult to change one without changing the other.

A key decision in the management of your worklife is whether your "primary" focus is the roles you prefer to play or the goals you seek to achieve.

Sometimes we need to adapt our goals to the roles, and sometimes the roles to the goals. The reason many people fail to achieve their goals, or become hopelessly frustrated in their lives and work, is because they do not take the time to decide what they really want and what they are willing to do for it, and recognize what the trade-offs will be.

The Issue

Have you ever set a goal, then failed to achieve it and couldn't figure out why? Have you ever made a promise to be the best at something (spouse, parent, friend, sibling, employee, manager) but found you could not live up to the level of excellence you wanted to achieve? Did it leave you feeling less than fulfilled? What you experienced is the inevitable dichotomy between roles and goals. What is important to recognize is that roles and goals are inextricably tied together. Here is an example of the conflict expressed by a client.

Work/Career	**Roles I play**
	Regional Manager
	Goals I've set
	1. *Become a vice-president in 10 years*
Personal Relations	**Roles I play**
	Husband
	Father
	Goals I've set
	1. *Be actively involved with my children's school*

Do you see where there might be conflicts? Will the demands of the job allow him the time to be the best spouse and parent? Will his personal definition of "best" be aligned with his spouse and children's definition of "best"? In his efforts to achieve all these goals, can he maintain a balance? This may be your challenge as you identify your Roles and Goals.

The following worksheet will help you recognize what roles you are presently playing in each of your Life facets. You will then determine what goals you have set or intend to set in those roles. The final step will be to assess whether your goals for your Life Facet of Work/Career conflict with your other goals.

Instructions: For each Life Facet specified in the left-hand column, list all the important roles you frequently play. (Listed in parentheses are some examples of roles to help you get started.) Then identify your top three goals. You may not have specific goals in each area.

If this exercise makes you think of a potential goal, record it, but don't worry about declaring goals to simply fill in the empty space. It is also helpful to keep in mind that although you may be ambitious and want to accomplish a lot, a focused and reasonable goal will typically help you stay the course. When working on new goals, studies have shown that we can psychologically handle approximately a 10 percent change at a time before stress begins to occur. Remember, you can always add more later.

Work/Career

(Examples: manager, entertainer, engineer, mentor, stay-at-home parent, accountant, nurse, mechanic, homemaker, landscaper, etc.)

Roles I play
_____
_____
_____

Goals I've set
1. _____
2. _____
3. _____

Personal Relations

(Examples: parent, spouse, son, daughter, uncle, aunt, grandparent, significant other, pet owner, etc.)

Roles I play
_____
_____
_____

Goals I've set
1. _____
2. _____
3. _____

Health and Fitness

(Examples: healthy eater, weight watcher, baseball player, coach, tennis player, exerciser, etc.)

Roles I play
_____
_____
_____

Goals I've set
1. _____
2. _____
3. _____

Personal Growth

(Examples: student, reader, self-learner, thinker, explorer, meditater, etc.)

Roles I play
_____
_____
_____

Goals I've set
1. _____
2. _____
3. _____

Spiritual

(Examples: religious member, prayer circle participant, choir member, spiritual book reader, lay minister, etc.)

Roles I play
_____
_____
_____

Goals I've set
1. _____
2. _____
3. _____

Citizenship

(Examples: activist, volunteer, community leader, community group board member, etc.)

Roles I play
_____
_____
_____

Goals I've set
1. _____
2. _____
3. _____

Economic

(Examples: saver, financial manager, bill payer, investor, buyer, etc.)

Roles I play
_____
_____
_____

Goals I've set
1. _____
2. _____
3. _____

Play

(Examples: sport player, card player, computer gamer, moviegoer, TV watcher, swimmer, etc.)

Roles I play
_____
_____
_____

Goals I've set
1. _____
2. _____
3. _____

Now that you have identified your goals in all aspects of your life, let's look at possible conflicts with your goals for your Work/Career. In this part of the exercise, you will need to again review your prioritization of your Life Facets from chapter 2, p. 21. Are they still the same?

Instructions: In the following exercise, start by listing your Work/Career goals (the first Life Facet) in order of importance. Then, working with the seven remaining Life Facets, indicating your key goal for each area and any potential conflicts between that goal and your work/career goals. Reflecting back on the example in the introduction to this exercise, do you see any potential conflicts relative to your Work/Career goals?

My Work/Career goals in order of importance are:

1. _____

2. _____

3. _____

Life Facet - Personal Relations

Goal _____

Potential conflicts with my Work/Career goals: _____

_____

_____

Life Facet - Health and Fitness

Goal _____

Potential conflicts with my Work/Career goals: _____

_____

_____

Life Facet - Personal Growth

Goal _____

Potential conflicts with my Work/Career goals: _____

_____

_____

Life Facet - Spiritual

Goal _____

Potential conflicts with my Work/Career goals: _____

_____

_____

Life Facet - Citizenship
Goal _____
Potential conflicts with my Work/Career goals: _____
_____
_____

Life Facet - Economic
Goal _____
Potential conflicts with my Work/Career goals: _____
_____
_____

Life Facet - Play
Goal _____
Potential conflicts with my Work/Career goals: _____
_____
_____

Answer the following questions to further explore possible conflicts and ensure you have goals you can and want to achieve.

    Are there issues with time and resources?

    Do I have balance?

    Is there agreement between my goals?

    Do other important individuals in my life share these goals?

Are my goals in alignment with my "**being**, **doing** and **having**"?

Do all these goals energize me?

Do any of my roles conflict with my goals or vice versa?

Do these goals express my values —- do they have me "walk my talk"?

One last thought about goals. In any goal setting effort, it is recommended that you set "stretch goals," goals that seem difficult or that you haven't a clue how to achieve, to challenge yourself. However, if the goal is too far a stretch, in conflict with other goals, or interferes with basic needs (Chapter 3, Motivators) you will become too frustrated and give up. Our goal is for you to challenge yourself enough to derive energy and joy from the possibility and the journey involved in achieving your goals, not set yourself up for stress and a sense of defeat.

Roles and Goals – Analysis and Reflection

Instructions: These are coaching questions, a means of reflecting on this exercise for greater insight. We recommend you review them and write down your thoughts.

1. What reaction did you have after looking at your Roles and Goals?

2. How do you feel about your work/career goals overall?

3. What insights did you gain about your goals overall?

4. What conflicts, if any, did you see in achieving your work/career goals?

5. What changes do you need to make in achieving your roles and goals?

6. Are your goals enough of a stretch to challenge you? Or are they too much?

Finding Your Joy

It's time to clarify your purpose, recognize your dream work, and get one step closer to transforming your dream into reality.

If you have read this far and completed all of the exercises, you are ready. To stop now would be an insult to you and the effort you have made to define the person you want to be. This is a critical point, since it is the last exercise you will complete before making significant decisions on future actions to create joy in what you do.

The magic formula is: Your purpose, which gives you *power* + your dream that inspires *passion* = the right fit resulting in *joy*! This is what life is all about; understanding what your Life Purpose is, using that, plus all the other aspects to define your Dream Work, and thus realize joy. This is your **be**, **do** and **have**.

You will begin by writing your Life Purpose Statement. In chapters 3, 4 and 5, you looked at your Life Purpose relative to **being**, **doing** and **having**. Now it is time to pull them all together. Your Life Purpose Statement answers the question, "What will bring my life meaning?" "Why am I here?" and "What can I do to bring value to the world?"

In this statement, you will recognize who you are, what you are good at doing and like to do, and your values. From a business perspective, your Life Purpose Statement serves as the mission and vision statement for your life, and can help you navigate decision making and change. It can help you determine if you are on course, and when it may be time to reassess one of the components of **being, doing** and **having**. From there, armed with your Life Purpose, you will design your Dream Work. This is your opportunity. Go for it!

Life Purpose Statement

Instructions: Write the statements or ideas you drafted in chapters 3, 4 and 5 for **being**, **doing** and **having**.

My Life Purpose Statement would include the following to embrace my *being*:

_____

_____

My Life Purpose Statement would include the following to accentuate my *doing*:

_____

_____

My Life Purpose Statement would include the following to create my *having*:

_____

_____

Instructions: Reflect on and answer the following questions.

How do your **being**, **doing** and **having** statements support each other?

What is the common theme?

What, if anything, could be contradictory?

What, if anything, is missing?

Instructions: Now you are ready to write one statement that is representative of what you want to base your life on from this day forward. This final Life Purpose Statement will be your source of measurement; you can use it to compare decisions you make and actions you take to see if you are on course.

This (preferably) one sentence statement could be the answer to the question, "If I was at the end of my life, how would I know that I am fulfilled?" Your Life Purpose Statement is how you will know that your life has meaning and if you are on track. It is the inheritance that you leave to the world.

We thought this would be a good opportunity to give you examples of Life Purpose Statements by sharing our own.

> **Prudence** — "I am always a caring, insightful and loving person who uses her God-given gifts to support people in finding joy in work. As I do this I will have success in my work and accomplish my goals."

> **Mary** — "As a compassionate, determined and innovative woman of service, I offer my gifts of curiosity and creativity. I am dedicated to contributing to the evolution of concrete and abstract systems for purposes of improving individual, group and community health, as well as my family's and my own."

> **Bob** — "As a teacher, writer, speaker and mentor, I influence everyone I meet to experience harmony with the people, processes, environment and systems at their places of work and play, and in their homes and communities, so they will live joyful lives."

My LIFE PURPOSE STATEMENT is:

_____
_____
_____
_____
_____

While this statement may change with major life transitions, *live it like it is forever.*

Dream Work

"The poorest man is not without a cent but without a dream."

—Unknown

One last step in pursuing the work that is going to bring you joy is to dream a little. If you think back to when you were writing the stories from your childhood, did you remember any dreams you had? Did you dream of being a policeman or fireman because they were people you could look up to? Were you enthralled by the adventures of the astronauts, or did you love to play teacher or nurse? Did you dream of being a movie star or playing professional sports? What happened to those dreams? Are you done with them, or are they still valid in some way?

Now we want you to dream from the perspective of your Life Purpose Statement, what you know about yourself and your interests, skills, abilities and desires. Set aside all the practical obstacles that could be in your way and just let yourself dream. You could answer the question, "What career or job would I wish for if I was granted one wish? "If I could live my life over from the beginning, what would I be doing now?" What has everyone said you would be perfect at and you agree with them? The only stipulation in your dreaming is to make it relevant to you!

In my Dream Work I would:

Be _____
_____
_____

Do _____
_____
_____

Have _____
_____
_____

Instructions: Now answer the following questions to take a closer look at your Dream Work.

What would prevent you from achieving your Dream Work?

How does your Life Purpose Statement align with your Dream Work?

What one step could you take to get closer to your Dream Work?

How does your Dream Work align with the work you *do* now?

How do you demonstrate your Character Traits and Personal Style in your Dream Work?

What motivations are you responding to?

What Aptitudes and Skills do you utilize in your Dream Work?

How can you do your Dream Work in a Work Environment that is consistent with your True Values?

Which True Values are in alignment with your Dream Work?

What opportunities do you see in your present Work Environment that aligns with your Dream Work?

Life Purpose and Dream Work – Analysis and Reflection

Instructions: These are coaching questions, a means of reflecting on this exercise for greater insight. We recommend your review them and write down your thoughts.

1. **What reaction did you have to writing your Life Purpose Statement?**

2. **How does your Life Purpose Statement align with the work that you do now?**

3. **How do you feel about your Dream Work?**

4. **What insights did you gain about the relationship of your Life Purpose Statement to your Dream Work?**

5. **What changes would you like to make to your current work situation relative to your Life Purpose Statement?**

6. **What opportunities do you see to realize your Life Purpose Statement and your Dream Work? What is your first step?**

"The habit of always putting off an experience until you can afford it, or until the time is right, or until you know how to do it, is one of the greatest burglars of joy. Be deliberate, but once you've made up your mind - jump in."

— Charles R.Swindoll

"Every job is a self-portrait of the person who did it. Autograph your work with excellence."

— Unknown

7

Ready, Set, Go!

Now that you know what you want, let's breathe some life into it! In developing your plan, you will be assessing, analyzing and reflecting on the conclusions you have made and recognizing your commitment. We are well aware that now that the end is in sight, you may be anxious to zoom to the finish line, but we want to encourage you to complete the journey.

To put the wheels of **making it happen** into motion, you will complete the following exercises:

- **Career Plan**

  Have you ever wondered why you haven't achieved your goals? It may be because you haven't taken the necessary steps to get there. *Goals without a plan remain dreams.* Putting together a Career Plan is your opportunity to be clear about what you want and what it is going to take to get there. It is about recognizing that goals have a greater chance of being accomplished when measurable, progressive steps are identified with appropriate time frames and support systems. In other words, goals can be accomplished if you know what you are looking for, what you need to do to get there, and by when. While you may not like to plan, think of this as your opportunity to get real and be the force of your actions.

- **Work Template**

  A Work Template is your final step of clarity about what you want. Whether you are clear that you need to leave your current work situation and look for a new job, or you want to move to a new area of responsibility within you current organization, your Work Template is a process to put into words what you want and to recognize it when you see it. It should be viewed as the precursor for an active job search.

Career Plan

It can be intimidating to think about a Career Plan. You may be having thoughts like, "How can you know what will happen in the future?" "What if I change my mind about my goals?" or "I have never planned before, and everything has worked out."

Career planning is nothing more than identifying your goals and recognizing what it will take to get there. You plan all the time, whether it is for projects at work or tasks at home. Your plan can be extremely detailed, or a general outline. In either case, it will put you into action. You have probably heard the saying, "Fail to plan, plan to fail." Without a plan, you may not fail, but you will not achieve all that is possible.

Developing a Career Plan is about getting into action regarding your work and career goals. To develop a Career Plan is to take responsibility for your career and make it happen! In the Introduction, you were introduced to five key messages:

If you don't care where you're going, it doesn't matter which way you go.

No one is coming.

You don't have to do anything you don't want to do, except die.

Life is full of trade-offs.

There is no failure, only feedback.

Your Career Plan is your response to these messages.

To begin planning, you first need to be clear about your goals. You have identified goals relative to your roles, you have crafted your Life Purpose Statement, and you have defined your Dream Work. Now we want you to translate that into work and career goals. To ensure your goals are relevant and meaningful, we use the SMART-VS goal setting formula. SMART-VS stands for Specific, Measurable, Attainable, Relevant, and Timing - Visible and Supported.

As you fill in the career-planning chart, you should be asking yourself the following questions:

Specific — *Are my goals in alignment with my purpose, interests, skills and abilities?* This question helps you apply your maximum power with effective effort to achieve what you want.

Measurable — *Can the achievement of my goals be measured? What is the measurement criterion?* You will want to have small checkpoints, particularly with large goals, to keep your interest up and your passion engaged.

Attainable — *Can my goals be accomplished?* This is an opportunity to recognize what you directly have control over. Wishful thinking can be fun but can sap your energy if you spend too much of your time waiting; no energy, no power, absolutely no possibility of passion or joy.

Relevant — *Is this what I want to spend my time doing, and will I feel elated and energized when I have achieved it? Does this support your Life Purpose and Dream Work?* If a goal is relevant to your desire, it will lead directly to creating joy.

Timing — *By when will I hold myself accountable to achieve this goal?* Procrastination and avoidance are a signal that lets you know you need to reassess something. If you do not heed "their" warning signals, you can sap yourself of power, passion and joy. Once this kind of negativity has become associated with your goal, it is very hard to get yourself back in the game.

Later, you will address the issue of your making your goals **Visible** and **Supported** to further ensure you achieve them.

Instructions: Enter your work and career goals in the following table. You can have as many goals as you like. However if you have too many, you can not only become overwhelmed and stressed, but unfocused. Try for a maximum of three significant goals. Also, if you have chosen goals that are more than five years away, you may want to develop interim goals to keep you energized and in action.

Work and Career Goal Chart

Career Goal	Measurement	Timing (M/D/Y)	Attainable (Y/N)	Relevant (Y/N

Creating Your Career Plan

Your Career Plan is a way of creating a structure to achieve and make your goals more than just a wish or dream. There are a variety of planning methods that you can use to create your own Career Plan. One method is expressed in the phrase from Steven Covey — "begin with the end in mind" (Covey 1989, p.98). Imagine that you have achieved your goal and you are now looking back over all the actions you had to take to get there. In this exercise, you move backward through your actions, asking yourself at each step, "What would I have to have done, and by when, for this result to occur?"

Here is an example:
(Hint: If you read from the bottom of the table up, you will see the progression.)

Action	By when
Goal: Assume responsibility as (role) for (area of responsibility)	**Date:** March 1
Prior action: Successfully interview for (role/responsibility)	**Date:** February 16
Prior action: Identified as a candidate for (role/responsibility)	**Date:** January 16
Prior action: Apply for (role/responsibility)	**Date:** November 15
Prior action: Identify candidate qualifications for (role/responsibility)	**Date:** October 30
Prior action: Discuss interest in (role/responsibility) with supervisor.	**Date:** October 15
Prior action: Understand process in company for selecting candidates for (role/responsibility)	**Date:** September 30
Prior action: Recognize interest in new (role/responsibility)	**Date:** September 1

Now it is your turn. This is your opportunity to take responsibility for what you want and go after it. Think through what it is going to take to accomplish a goal and use the following chart to record your actions.

Action	By when
Goal:	**Date:**
Prior action:	**Date:**
Prior action:	**Date:**
Prior action:	**Date:**
Prior action:	**Date:**
Prior action:	**Date:**
Prior action:	**Date:**
Prior action:	**Date:**
Prior action:	**Date:**
Prior action:	**Date:**
Prior action:	**Date:**
Prior action:	**Date:**

These are the last steps to make your goals a reality, making them Visible and finding Support.

Visible — *What can I do to keep myself focused on this goal? How can I remind myself that this is what I want?* By making a goal visible in some way, you add additional energy to achieving it.

Supported — *Who can help me?* Support can be as little as being reminded of what we desire and want to achieve or it can be actual assistance in one or many of the steps to your goal.

Instructions:
Create signs or small banners of your goals and post them in places where you will see them often. You can cut out pictures, or strategically place symbols that are physical reminders of where you are going. While this might seem like an trivial step, it will get you closer to making your goals real. *Just having the constant reinforcement of seeing your goals can cause you to work toward the goal without any thought or intent.* Consider the following question:

Where can you post your goals so you will see them?

While many of us believe we can accomplish much on our own, most of our true success comes from the help and support of others. We live in a world of connections, teams, colleagues and families. Engaging support can not only help, but prevent resistance. Support will be in two forms: to discuss it and share thoughts and ideas, and to hold you accountable in a *loving and supportive way*.

This is a great opportunity to work with a mentor. A mentor is someone who, because of their experience and position, can provide you with additional insight and knowledge. True mentors become committed to your success, and thus are natural support structures to help keep you moving forward toward your goals. To find support, consider the following questions:

Who would have an interest in helping you achieve your goals?

Who, because of their position and experience, might make a good mentor?

Once you have chosen a support person and they have agreed, suggest a regular schedule of meetings, maybe once a month. At these meetings, your support person functions as a sounding board about your goal and plan. Commit to accomplishing some specific action by your next meeting. If you need encouragement to keep moving forward, you might ask them to check in with you periodically to reinforce your accomplishments and offer help.

Warning! The role of your support person is support, not to make you feel guilty if something happens which prevents you from keeping your commitment. That can and will happen. Your support person is also not there to hold you up, or be a substitute for your own power or passion. You are responsible for the actions and inactions of your life even as you receive help. Your support person can help you look at what is getting in the way and what you can do to address it.

One last thought................YOU CAN DO IT!

Career Plan – Analysis and Reflection

Instructions: These are coaching questions, a means of reflecting on this exercise for greater insight. We recommend you review them and write down your thoughts.

1. What reaction did you have to developing a Career Plan?

2. Are you surprised by the goals you set?

3. What insights did you gain about your current work situation and your goals?

4. How would you feel if you did not achieve your goals?

5. Do you have any support issues?

6. What obstacles will you face as you implement your Career Plan?

Work Template

We believe that at this point, you have enough information to find your ideal work. To clarify what this might look like, we will help you prepare a Work Template. A template is a guide or pattern to hold up against your current position, or any position you are considering, to determine, "Will this opportunity fulfill me?" "Is this what I *want* to do?" Think of this as identifying your target market, or your marketing plan to go after the right opportunities within your current organization. This template will serve foundationally to help you organize your thoughts for any interview you may attend or resumé you create. It should speak to your Life Purpose and your Dream Work and clarify how they support the achievement of your goals.

If you have decided to leave your current organization, we recognize that you may want to jump to creating a resumé as a proactive and critical step in finding that new position. Ultimately, we all need to have an up-to-date resumé. However, what is going to improve and accelerate your job search is the preparatory work you have done while developing your Living Career Portfolio, and the way this process has ignited your passion for what you are now choosing to do and how it is that you are choosing to do it.

In your Work Template, you will answer the following questions:

> What work do I feel passionate about?
> What talents do I want to utilize in my work?
> What are the values that I need to express in my work?
> What do I need from my employer?
> What environment will work for me?

Recognize that in the following exercise you will be referring to what you have already completed in chapters 2 through 6.

How to Use Your Work Template
As we have said, your Work Template is a means of being clear about what you want and having a means to evaluate any opportunities you are considering. It will also provide information you need to create your resumé and prepare for job possibilities. It will help you develop your questions for any job interviews and negotiate for any job.

Where Are You Today?
Now is also the time to take another look at your Work Health Assessment. We strongly recommend you walk through your Work Health Assessment again and look at whether your responses have changed. Completing this review prior to creating your Work Template will help you recognize some of the shifts and changes you may have made in your perspective and your increased knowledge and awareness of what you now want in your work life.

Instructions: Review the following components of the Work Template and then complete the worksheet.

> **My Passion:** This is what you want to do, what will fulfill you. This can be the objective statement on a resumé. This is what will bring you *passion, power* and *joy*.
>
> You have worked actively with Your Stories from chapter 2. Begin by reflecting on your history through Your Stories. What have you accomplished in the past that still has meaning for you? Which one or two stories have the most meaning? What kind of work do they represent? Turn to your Life Purpose Statement created in chapter 6 on page 110. What does that tell you about your work? Reflect on your Life Interests from chapter 3 on page 34-36.
>
> **My Talents:** Recognizing and being able to use our talents motivates us to achieve a level of performance that brings satisfaction and accomplishment. What are your prized talents, skills and abilities that you want to utilize in your work? These are your job qualifications, i.e., what you have to offer to an employer. Realize that you have been given these talents as gifts, and that you have a responsibility to utilize them.
>
> Begin by reviewing the Character Traits from chapter 3 on page 42 that serve you the best. Now look at the Aptitudes and Skills you identified in chapter 4 on pages 61-62. What aptitudes were you born with that so interested you to develop skills around them? In recognizing your Personal Style in chapter 3 on page 51, how will the way you work, in both easy and trying times, provide you with the opportunity for success?
>
> **My Values:** Our True Values are the compass for our life. Values in alignment with our work ensure a sense of well-being. Values out of alignment cause discomfort and pain, and for many people can result in illness. When you identified your top seven internal values in chapter 5 on page 82, you put a stake in the ground around how you want to live your life, including at work. Another aspect of values is the recognition of the values of our employer. How do they appear to the world, and what do they profess as the values they follow? What might your Personal Style indicate about what you value and how you see your world? Which values would be complementary to yours? Which ones might seem totally foreign?
>
> **My Needs:** Are you clear about what you need? This is usually the practical aspect of why we work. But sometimes it can be more complicated as we connect our needs with our True Values, Roles and Goals, Life Interests, etc. Refer back to chapter 3 on page 50, where you summarized your needs as motivators. What are your current needs, and therefore your motivation? How does your motivation align with the specifics of your current goals? As you consider your needs, take into account where you are at the *basic level* (physiological, safety, control and power) versus the *higher level* (esteem, love, self-actualization, manifested actualization or transcendence*)*. In the process of completing the template, you may begin to see new possibilities for meeting your basic needs that will also allow you to work toward meeting your higher needs.
>
> On your template, look at your **basic needs** for compensation and benefits. What do you want in compensation and what do you need? You can consider this from the standpoint of your lifestyle and responsibilities, or as an issue of recognition and how you are valued. Your benefits package can also be a significant portion of your compensation. What benefits do you require?

For your **higher needs,** consider the question of opportunities and what you want from your work or career over the long-term. What have you learned about yourself and what motivates you? Do you have a desire to climb the career ladder? Do you want to be able to move to other locations? Do you want to earn larger sums of money, or have the opportunity to increase your skills with training and experience? Do you want to be able to do other work?

My Environment: From the discoveries you made in chapter 5 about your Preferred Employer on pages 84-88 and Work Environment on pages 91-93, you can define the environment that is going to work best for you. You should also take a look at your Life Facets in chapter 2 on page 21, to factor in what relationship your work will have with the other interests in your life.

Rating
Will you find the perfect job match? We would like to say yes, but chances are you will find a job with a few aspects that don't measure up. Maybe the actual work is what you want and the opportunities are there, but the money isn't satisfactory. Or maybe you have to relocate when you would rather stay in the same area. Whatever your issue, only you can evaluate what is most important to you and decide what you are willing to make a trade off.

The last step in preparing your Work Template is to give each aspect a rating of importance to you at this point in time. You need to realize that things change, and what is important to you today may not be in a few years from now. Using a scale of 1 to 5, with **1 being the most important**, rate each of the five areas of your Work Template. You are not ranking these areas successively, but note if you have given them the same ranking. What does this tell you about your expectations for yourself and for your happiness?

Work Template

This template is my opportunity to reflect on any position I am considering and assess whether it is going to allow me to be motivated about what I do, be aware when I have power to make a change, and provide me with the opportunity to feel passion around my job and find joy in my work.

My Passion   Rating _____

If I were in a position that fulfilled me, I would be _____
_____
_____

My Talents   Rating _____

The traits I am comfortable with and would need to express in my work are _____
_____

It is important for me to utilize the aptitudes and skills I have by _____

My style would show up at work as _____

My Values   Rating _____

I cannot work in an environment that does not support _____

I would want the company I work for to value _____

My Needs   Rating _____

I *need* to be paid a salary in the range of _____

I would *like* to be paid a salary in the range of _____

The benefits I *must* have are _____

The benefits I would *like* to have are _____

The opportunities I would like to have are _____

Other forms of compensation I would consider _____

My Environment   Rating _____

The leadership style that I work best with is _____
_____
_____

The organizational work style that is best for me is _____
_____

I am the happiest and most successful when the people I work with are _____
_____

I need my physical surroundings to be _____
_____

Based on my current priorities, my time commitment to my work is _____
_____

Work Template – Analysis and Reflection

Instructions: These are coaching questions, a means of reflecting on this exercise for greater insight. We recommend you review them and write down your thoughts.

1. What does your Work Template reveal to you about your current position?

2. What did the rating of each area of your Work Template reveal?

3. How does your template support your career goals and/or dream job?

4. What changes would you make in your resumé to align it with your Work Template?

5. What is the feasibility of what you have outlined in your Work Template?

6. What has changed in your answers on the Work Health Assessment?

"Intellectual growth should commence at birth and cease only at death."

— Albert Einstein

"Upon the subject of education, not presuming to dictate any plan or system respecting it, I can only say that I view it as the most important subject which we as a people may be engaged in."

— Abraham Lincoln

Your Credentials, Please!

Gathering – Training and Education

You will begin in earnest to complete your own Living Portfolio in this chapter. In the next six chapters, you will be collecting all of your evidence of your work history. As we suggested in the Introduction, you may want to set up a binder so that all your materials are in one location. Then, no matter which direction your work life takes, or what may come up, you will be ready!

Credentials are the result of your education and training. You will be gathering and describing all of your credentials in this chapter. You may have completed certifications, as well as attended workshops, seminars or programs that identify your competencies. This chapter covers all of your education, including company sponsored internal training programs and education for personal growth.

Your credentials are important and can fill in gaps relative to your Dream Work. Do you know if you have the right training and education, or could you use more? What was the purpose of your training and education? Is it a requirement in the field you are looking at entering? Also, as you have seen throughout this book, the details of your experience often provide clues to who you are.

Collect your credentials. They represent your history. It is a good idea to make professional photocopies of your degrees and certificates sized to place in your portfolio. Make sure to maintain a corresponding file for your original documents so you can access them if requested.

- **Formal Education and Training**
  You will identify all of your education and training including that which you received at school as well as on the job.

- **Self-Development**
  You will be creating a list of all the self-development you have completed. This would include classes you have attended, online courses, self-improvement initiatives, self-directed study, developmental videos, listening to tapes, etc. Hidden interests are often revealed in what we choose for self-development.

We recommend you gather all of your information. Now is *not* the time to censor it, particularly around self-development. You never know how the little things you ***do*** add up to supporting what you want. If you are ***doing*** these things strictly for yourself, they will surely address your interests, values and priorities, and give you important clues about your desires. Once you have completed the process, you can streamline the information with respect to your current objective.

Formal Education and Training

Instructions: Begin organizing your thoughts and information here. Include the following information:

- ⇨ Name of degree, program, or class
- ⇨ Dates of study
- ⇨ Institution
- ⇨ Address
- ⇨ Learning, skill or experience gained

Name _____ Dates _____

Institution _____

Address _____

Learning, skills or experience gained _____

Name _____ Dates _____

Institution _____

Address _____

Learning, skills or experience gained _____

Name _____ Dates _____

Institution _____

Address _____

Learning, skills or experience gained _____

Self-Development

Instructions: Begin organizing your thoughts and information here. Include the following information:

- ⇨ Name of activity, class, program
- ⇨ Dates of study
- ⇨ Source
- ⇨ Address
- ⇨ Learning, skill or experience gained

Name _____ Dates _____

Source _____

Address _____

Learning, skills or experience _____

Name _____ Dates _____

Source _____

Address _____

Learning, skills or experience _____

Name _____ Dates _____

Source _____

Address _____

Learning, skills or experience _____

Formal Education and Self-Development – Analysis and Reflection

Instructions: These are coaching questions, a means of reflecting on this exercise for greater insight. We recommend you review them and write down your thoughts.

1. Does your education align with your current direction (Life Facets, Life Purpose Statement, Dream Work, Career Plan, Work Template)?

2. Do you have enough education to be competitive in the work environment and achieve your goals?

3. What life interests, goals, and values are reflected in your self-development?

4. How do you feel about what you have accomplished in your education and self-development?

5. Is there anything else you would like to achieve in your education?

6. Is there any research or investigation you need to do regarding your education and career goals?

"When your work speaks for itself, don't interrupt."

— Henry J. Kaiser

"One machine can do the work of fifty ordinary men. No machine can do the work of one extraordinary man."

— Elbert Hubbard

Highlighting Your Work

Gathering – Work Examples

Your collection of work examples can be an important part of your portfolio and a powerful sales tool in your job search. Work examples are demonstrations of your competencies and skills, and can provide an employer with a preview of your capabilities.

The results of the exercises in chapters 3 and 4 can help you identify what you want to highlight. This is where you demonstrate "walking your talk"— how you have realized your Life Interests, Character Traits, Personal Style, Aptitudes and Skills into tangible accomplishments. Be sure you are prepared to discuss what competencies and skills are being demonstrated by your work.

- **Work Examples**

  You will gather work examples such as projects, presentations, and reports that demonstrate your work abilities and skills, from both current and former employers. Update this material regularly with new examples.

  You can organize this section by job title or job description with supporting examples, or by an aptitude or skill, such as "Leadership," with project examples or personal outcomes. You could also choose to represent what you have done for a particular organization or group of people to demonstrate your interests. Be creative, and pick the best of what you have accomplished.

Work Examples

Instructions: Begin organizing your thoughts and information here. Include the following information:

- ⇨ Title and description
- ⇨ Reason for including example
- ⇨ Value to employer (outcomes, benefits, results)
- ⇨ History
- ⇨ Roles performed and skills demonstrated

Special Note: Recognize whether any work you are including contains information confidential to an employer. Either censor it or do not include it.

Title and description

Reason

Value

History

Roles and skills

Title and description

Reason

Value

History

Roles and skills

Title and description

Reason

Value

History

Roles and skills

Work Examples – Analysis and Reflection

Instructions: These are coaching questions, a means of reflecting on this exercise for greater insight. We recommend you review them and write down your thoughts.

1. What observations can you make about your work examples?

2. What additional skills, talents and interests did you discover in your work examples?

3. What skills are not demonstrated by your work examples?

4. How do you feel about the quality of work you are including?

5. How do your work examples support your goals?

6. As you reflect upon your work examples do you see power, passion and joy?

"All know that the drop merges into the ocean but few know that the ocean merges into the drop."

— Kahir

In Honor of Recognition

Gathering – Awards and Honors

Awards and honors demonstrate where you and your work have been exceptional. They can be from an employer or employment situation, from another organization, or from an individual. The community may have honored you for your talents and contributions. You may have been honored or recognized as a member of a group or team. What is important is that awards and honors speak to your character and your accomplishments.

Recognition is evidence of ***being*** appreciated for who you are and what you ***do***, and provides further support for what you can accomplish. This can come in many forms, so we ask that you be creative in your thinking. You can include thank-you notes and letters of acknowledgement of an achievement. If there was an event held in your honor, for example, you may include a press copy of the event, or a program.

- **Awards and Honors**
  You will be gathering *all* the awards and honors you have received. In some cases, you may be able to include the actual documents or photocopies. Remember to think about the times you were mentioned or honored in the slightest way — this is not the time to be modest! Did you ever receive a monetary award for your achievements? How about a t-shirt, coffee mug or book to recognize performance? Look past the obvious.

Awards and Honors

Instructions: Begin organizing your thoughts and information here. You may want to take a photograph if the award is in the form of a trophy or plaque. Include the following information:

- ⇨ Name of award or honor
- ⇨ Involvement and contribution
- ⇨ Source and contact information

Once again, do not start by eliminating information. Collect everything, and then choose which information to leave in your portfolio and which to put in an auxiliary file.

Name

Involvement and contribution

Source and contact information

Name

Involvement and contribution

Source and contact information

Name

Involvement and contribution

Source and contact information

Awards and Honors - Analysis and Reflection

Instructions: These are coaching questions, a means of reflecting on this exercise for greater insight. We recommend you review them and write down your thoughts.

1. What did you observe about the awards and honors you have received?

2. What awards and/or honors are you most proud of?

3. What were the conditions that led to the awards and honors you are most proud of?

4. Based on your awards and honors, how would you describe your interests?

5. What award or honor would you like to receive as a result of who you are and what you offer?

6. How do the results of this chapter make you feel about your direction?

"Whoever renders service to many puts himself in line for greatness — great wealth, great return, great satisfaction, great reputation and great joy."

— Jim Rohn

"We cannot seek achievement for ourselves and forget about progress and prosperity for our community...Our ambitions must be broad enough to include the aspirations and needs of others, for their sakes and for our own."

— Cesar Chavez

In Service to the Community

Gathering – Community Service

Volunteer projects can demonstrate your skills, competencies and values. Service often represents interests, aptitudes, or even talent that we do not demonstrate in our professional life. Since people do change jobs and careers, community service history can often provide clues to your next move.

Volunteerism can show employers that you take an active role in making valuable contributions, and not simply to be financially rewarded. Citizenship, ethics, values and the ability to have a multifaceted life can have an impact on employers when making hiring decisions. It also demonstrates that you are capable of implementing a strategy for creating balance, such that you will take on additional activities that are an important part of your True Values.

You will want to look at what your involvement means to you. Why have you volunteered and what might that indicate about you? How are these activities reflected in your Life Facets and Roles and Goals? What part of yourself and your commitments are you expressing? Also, don't discount how these activities provide networking sources for any job search. Consider whether any of your contacts may provide you with references or letters of recommendation. These contacts can become endorsements.

- **Community Activities**
 You will identify your community activities. You may have been active in your church or served as a scout leader. You may be a volunteer at the local hospital or school. You may sit on the board of some nonprofit organization or participate in organizing fundraisers. All these activities point to what you are interested in and what you are willing to commit yourself to.

Service to the Community

Community Activities

Instructions: Begin organizing your thoughts and information here. Include the following information:

- ⇨ Activity or organization
- ⇨ Type of involvement
- ⇨ Dates of involvement
- ⇨ Contact information

Name _____ Dates _____

Involvement _____

Contact _____

Name _____ Dates _____

Involvement _____

Contact _____

Name _____ Dates _____

Involvement _____

Contact _____

Community Activities – Analysis and Reflection

Instructions: These are coaching questions, a means of reflecting on this exercise for greater insight. We recommend you review them and write down your thoughts.

1. Do your community service activities match with who you have said you are? Do they match with what you are good at? Describe.

2. What do you think has motivated you to take part in these activities?

3. What skills, talents, interests and abilities are demonstrated and strengthened by your community service?

4. In what ways do you see performing these activities as being beneficial to you and an employer?

5. Which Character Traits, Motivators, True Values, and Life Facets does your involvement relate to?

6. What conclusion, if any, do you have about the type of community service you would like to do?

"Though it is important to stay focused, an occasional distraction can sometimes be a good thing. There is much value to be found in the unexpected. The people you didn't expect to meet, the places you didn't expect to go, the things you didn't expect to learn, can often lead you in new and positive directions."

— Ralph Marston

12 For Members

Gathering – Professional Memberships and Activities

Because you are committed to your work, you are likely a member of professional associations or involved in professional activities. Professional membership and service demonstrates commitment to your current or desired field. Participation provides an opportunity to obtain knowledge, experience, resources and networking support to keep up with your field's growing and changing knowledge and skill requirements. Active membership often implies to others that you are "active" and therefore current with your professional knowledge.

Professional membership can provide contacts for marketing, support and networking. In the process of making a job change, it is a great benefit to have a strong network within your field.

Your professional memberships can also speak highly of your Life Interests, and in some cases, the Work Environment you prefer. Your level of involvement can demonstrate how motivated you are within your chosen field and the match with your Character Traits, Personal Style, and Aptitudes and Skills. If work was a lower Life Facet priority (chapter 2), this section will also demonstrate that.

- **Professional Memberships and Activities**
  You will identify all the professional membership with which you have been involved. Be sure to include any special interest groups, as well as any acknowledgement or

recognition you may have received (which you also included in chapter 10). If you are an active member, you may have examples of work you have produced for the organization. These can be referenced here and kept with your work examples in chapter 9.

Professional Memberships and Activities

Instructions: Begin organizing your thoughts and information here. Include the following information:

- Organizations, including special interest groups
- Dates of involvement
- Participation and roles
- Contact information

Organization _____   Dates _____

Participation and roles _____

Contact _____

Organization _____   Dates _____

Participation and roles _____

Contact _____

Organization _____   Dates _____

Participation and roles _____

Contact _____

Professional Memberships – Analysis and Reflection

Instructions: These are coaching questions, a means of reflecting on this exercise for greater insight. We recommend you review them and write down your thoughts.

1. How active have you been in professional organizations?

2. Are there any organizations that you haven't joined that support your goals?

3. Do your professional memberships reflect your work goals?

4. What have been your reasons for being involved in organizations, or not being involved?

5. How have you participated in professional organizations?

6. How might you make better use of the benefits professional memberships may provide? What is your first step?

"Work is about daily meaning as well as daily bread. For recognition as well as cash; for astonishment rather than torpor; in short, for a sort of life rather than a Monday through Friday sort of dying... We have a right to ask of work that it include meaning, recognition, astonishment, and life."

— Studs Turkel

"Choose a job you love, and you will never have to work a day in your life."

— Confucious

Endorsing the Product (Yes, that's You!)

Gathering - References and Endorsements

This chapter is the evidence of how you are known. Your references are the individuals who can attest to your Character Traits, Personal Style, Aptitudes and Skills, and True Values. They can also provide evidence of where you have worked, and most importantly, your contributions.

It is typical to be asked for references with any job application or interview. References are sometimes requested for promotions, as well as in application for higher education and for most job applications. You will need three to five references an employer can check. You should select references that can address those abilities and characteristics you are emphasizing in your Work Template and resumé.

Another type of reference is an endorsement. It is valuable to get endorsements for who you are *being* and what you can *do*, and not just when you are seeking a job change. One type of endorsement is a performance review. It is always beneficial to get regular feedback on your performance. Even if your company does not have a formal review process, you can request feedback regarding your work as well as to find out how you can improve. Consider requesting feedback whenever you have been involved in projects or activities that are successful or deliver results for the company.

A thank-you is also a type of endorsement. Sometimes people forget to thank us for the work we do, and given time, will forget the details. It is okay to request feedback, and best to do it in a timely manner.

- **References and Endorsements**
References are the people who will give a positive recommendation about you to a potential employer or customer. In this exercise, you will start making a list of people who you would want as references and gather appropriate endorsements and recommendations. Do not leave references or endorsements to chance. All references should be interviewed so that you can be clear on what they will say about you to anyone who contacts them.

References and Endorsements

Instructions: Begin organizing your thoughts and information here. Include the following information:

⇨ Reference, name and title, or type of endorsement

⇨ Professional relationship

⇨ Contact information

⇨ Value as a reference or endorsement

Reference/endorsement _____

    Relationship _____

    Contact _____

Value _____

Reference/endorsement _____

    Relationship _____

    Contact _____

Value _____

Reference/endorsement _____

    Relationship _____

    Contact _____

Value _____

References and Endorsements – Analysis and Reflection

Instructions: These are coaching questions, a means of reflecting on this exercise for greater insight. We recommend you review them and write down your thoughts.

1. How do your references and endorsements support your work goals?

2. Do your references and endorsements reflect "the you" that you have described throughout this workbook?

3. What issues did you have in identifying references and endorsements?

4. What could you do to be more proactive regarding references and endorsements?

5. What is your reaction to "the story" this chapter tells about you?

6. What more would you like to do to obtain references and endorsements? What is your next step?

"The real tragedy of life is not in being limited to one talent, but in the failure to use that one talent."

— Edgar W. Work

"Discover the magic within yourself, dare to dream"

— Unknown

14 Is This the End?

Using Your Portfolio

When you are preparing for a new venture or exploring a potential opportunity, review all the information in your workbook. Your workbook and portfolio provides the evidence of what you want to **do** and why. You can use it in this capacity to apply for new positions, seek promotions, change careers, and be reminded of your magnificence.

If you are using it in a job interview, you may want to prepare extra copies to leave behind. View your portfolio as a sales tool, or an example of not only what you have accomplished, but what you *can* accomplish.

- **Customizing Your Portfolio**
  This is a good time for you to brainstorm your creative ideas. Ask yourself if there is information you may want to include that is not addressed in another chapter. You can include articles, both personal and general, or motivational information that illustrates your work and personal philosophies. You may want to include test scores, perhaps, or other miscellaneous reports that may be of interest to an employer.

If you have taken the dramatic step of creating your own web site, create printouts along with information to direct someone to its location! Or how about adding a list of books you have read, or places to which you have traveled? Include personal information that is important to you, and lets someone know who you are.

Keep It Current

It is important to review your portfolio just like you would your wardrobe or the maintenance of your home or automobile. Your portfolio needs to be kept current. Make sure all exercises are current and still represent you. If you keep your portfolio up to date, whether you find yourself in an unfortunate crisis, or perhaps in the face of a great opportunity, you will be ready and prepared. ***Finding Your Power, Passion and Joy Being At Work*** is a process that should be revisited to keep up with your growth and transformation. A body in motion stays in motion, and you will want to be able to keep up with yourself, being the best Mentor and Leader you can **be**.

Best wishes, and many blessings on your adventure!

Customizing Your Portfolio

Instructions: Begin organizing your thoughts and information here on what additions you want to make to your portfolio. Some ideas are:

- Quotes you live by
- Role models you look up to
- Personal accomplishments

Be creative!

Using Your Portfolio – Analysis and Reflection

Instructions: "We couldn't resist one last chance to coach you!

1. How complete is your Workbook and Portfolio?

2. Are you satisfied with the outcome? Why or why not?

3. Identify how this process can and has helped you in your life in general?

4. What are some of the ways in which you intend to use your Living Career Portfolio?

5. Who is responsible for your work life, and how do you know that?

6. Who else do you think this process could help, and how might you be able to be of service in making that happen?

Success

"Success is doing the best you can,
In as many ways as you can.
It is being just and honest and true —
Not in a few things, but in everything you do.

Always look ahead and never look back,
Believe you can make all your dreams come true.
Always believe in the best you can be
And have faith in the things that you do.

Forget about mistakes you've made yesterday,
The lessons you learn will prove valuable for today…
Never give up and think that you're through …
For there's always tomorrow and a chance to begin brand new.

It is in dreaming the greatest dreams …
And seeking the highest goals …
That we build the brightest tomorrows.

There is no limit to the goals you can attain,
Or the success you can achieve …
Your possibilities are as endless as your dreams.

Whatever it is that you seek in life,
Whatever our dreams and what you hope to achieve,
Whatever you try to reach-whatever you plan …
Can all be yours-if you only believe You Can!"

—Larry S. Chengges

Contacting Us

We would love to receive your questions, comments, or success stories, and can arrange to work with you on a more personal basis, should you be interested.

To Contact Mary
Mary Brandon, founder and president of **Aspect Consulting Inc.**, has more than a decade of notable experience in Employment Consulting, Program Design and Development and Motivation Coaching.

If you are interested in further exploring *why you* **do** what you **do**, or discovering if your free will and independent choice are truly operating, you don't have to **do** it alone. **Aspect Consulting, Inc.**, through non-threatening guiding techniques, has assisted its clients in making their search for often-elusive answers, easier—less frustrating and even fun.

To find a coaching program tailored to your specific personal needs, provide comment or inquire about services, or even share how your life is changing, you can email me at aspectconsulting@usa.net or go to MaryBrandon.com. The web site contains a list of my services and also an opportunity to receive my free tutorial. You can also take the Work Health Assessment (Chapter 2) and receive my personalized feedback and suggested plan.

To Contact Prudence
As the founder and president of being@work, I am thrilled and excited for you and the decision you made to find power, passion and joy in your work. Trust me, it can be done. I am also very grateful that you chose our book for your journey.

Please visit beingatwork.com or my blog beingatwork.blogs.com to see all the programs we sponsor and opportunities to get further assistance. You can send me a question via the web site and I will attempt to answer as many of the e-mails as I can. The web site also contains career and leadership stories which may be of help. You can also take the Work Health Assessment (Chapter 2) and receive feedback.

If you or your company are interested in leadership or work life coaching services, please contact me at pcole@beingatwork.biz or PrudenceCole.com

To Contact Bob
Bob has over forty years of experience in leadership and people development. He has been a keynote and motivational speaker, and a consultant in the areas of leadership, management, career counseling, change management, customer relations, and time management. He has trained thousands of people how to better manage their occupational and personal lives.

You can reach Bob through beingatwork.com, BobHunsberger.com or at his personal email address, thineagle@aol.com.

*We look forward to **being** at your service in the future!*

Appendix

Resources for Self-Assessment

For many additional recommended resources for self-assessment, go to powerpassionjoy.com

For personal development coaching, go to MaryBrandon.com

For executive leadership coaching go to PrudenceCole.com

BIBLIOGRAPHY

Bobgan, Martin and Barbara, *Four Temperaments; Astrology and Personality Testing*, Santa Barbara, CA, EastGate Publishers; 1992

de Broglie, Louis. *Heisenberg's Uncertainties and the Probabilistic Interpretation of Wave Mechanics: With Critical Notes of the Author (Fundamental Theories of Physics, Vol. 40)*. Boston: Kluwer Academic Publishers, 1991.

Butler, Tim and Waldroop, James. "Job Sculpting, the Art of Retaining Your Best People." *Harvard Business Review* (September-October 1999): 144-152.

Coelho, Paulo. *The Alchemist: A Fable About Following Your Dream.* New York: Harper Perennial, a division of Harper Collins Publishers, 1988.

Connelly, Sean, nomad4@gonewalkabout.com

Covey, Stephen. *The Seven Habits of Highly Effective People.* New York: Simon & Schuster, 1989.

Feinstein, PhD, David and Stanley Krippner, PhD. *The Mythic Path: Discovering the Guiding Stories of Your Past — Creating a Vision For Your Future.* New York: G.P. Putnam's Sons, 1997.

Forster, Mark. *How to Make Your Dreams Come True.* London: Holder & Stoughton, 2002.

Grabhorn, Lynn. *Excuse Me, Your Life is Waiting: The Astonishing Power of Feelings.* Charlottesville, VA: Hampton Roads Publishing Company, Inc., 2000.

Jones, Laurie Beth. *The Path: Creating Your Mission Statement for Work and for Life.* New York: Hyperion, 1996.

Judith, Anodea, PhD. *Wheels of Life: A User's Guide to the Chakra System*, 6th ed. St. Paul, MN: Llewellyn Publications, 2003.

Jung, Carl. *The Basic Writings of C.G. Jung*, edited, with an Introduction by Violet De Laszlo. New York: The Modern Library, 1959.

Maslow, Abraham H. *The Maslow Business Reader.* New York: Wiley, 2000.
———— *Maslow on Management,* revised ed.. New York:Wiley, 1998.

Myss, Caroline, PhD. *Anatomy of the Spirit: The Seven Stages of Power and Healing.* New York: Three Rivers Press, a division of Crown Publishers, 1996.
———— *Sacred Contracts: Awakening Your Divine Potential.* New York: Harmony Books, 2001.

Pearson, Carol S. *Awakening the Heroes Within: Twelve Archetypes to Help Us Find Ourselves and Transform our World.* New York: HarperCollins Publishers, 1991.

Bibliography

Sharp, Daryl. *Personality Types; Jung's Model of Typology.* Toronto: Inner City Books, 1987.

Sher, Barbara. *I Could Do Anything If Only I Knew What It Was: How to Discover What You Really Want and How to Get It.* New York: Bantam Doubleday Dell Publishing Group, Inc.,1994.
———— *Life You Love: In Ten Easy Step-by-Step Lessons.* New York:Bantam Doubleday Dell Publishing Group, Inc., 1996.

Sinetar, Marsha. *Do What You Love, The Money Will Follow: Discovering Your Right Livelihood.* New York: Dell Publishing, 1987.

Warren, Rick.. *The Purpose Driven Life: What on Earth am I Here For?* Grand Rapids, MI: Zondervan Publishing Company, 2002.

Index

A
Analysis and Reflection   2, 13, 19, 22, 25, 37, 43, 52, 55, 56, 63, 68, 73, 83, 89, 94, 98, 107, 113, 122, 128, 133, 137, 141, 146, 150, 154, 158
Aptitudes   59
Aptitudes and Skills   2, 57, 58, 59-63, 65, 66, 67, 68, 69, 112, 124, 135, 147, 151
Archetypes   44, 45, 162
Aspect Consulting   44, 160, 167
Awards and Honors   139-141

B
Be, do, have paradigm   xvii, 2, 53, 55, 58, 67, 76
Being   xvi, xix, 6, 11, 14, 23, 47, 53, 55, 56, 59, 64, 67, 69, 97, 98, 108, 109, 139, 151, 159
being@work   160, 167
Beliefs   21, 23 29, 53-54, 57, 65-66, 67, 76, 77, 95-96, 98
Butler, Timothy and James Waldroop   30

C
Career   2, 3, 6-11, 21, 30, 32, 33, 43, 64, 77, 83, 95, 99, 101-102, 104, 105, 107, 111, 117, 118, 125, 128, 133, 143, 155, 160, 165, 167
Career Plan   2, 115, 117, 119, 122, 133
Career Portfolio   xvii, xviii, 2, 123, 155-158
Categorization   29
Character Traits   2, 29, 38-43, 44, 53-55, 65, 112, 124, 135, 146, 147, 151
Characters   44, 45, 47, 50-52
Colleagues   8, 11, 30, 81, 90, 91,92, 94, 121
Community activities   144, 145-146
Community service   143, 146
Confidentiality   136
Covey, Stephen   27, 119, 162
Credentials   90, 129, 131, 133

D
Doing   xix, 6, 7, 10, 23, 53, 57, 58, 64, 67-68, 69 97, 98, 108, 109, 118, 130
Dream Work   2, 58, 100, 108, 111-113, 117, 118, 123, 129, 133

E
Education   10, 11, 77, 81, 97, 129-131, 133, 151
Employer   2, 8, 30, 70, 73, 75-76, 77, 83, 84-89, 95-96, 123-127, 135, 136, 139, 143, 146, 151, 152, 155
Employment history   8, 68, 73
Endorsements   143, 151-154
Environment   2, 5, 9, 33, 75-76, 77, 81, 84, 90-94, 95, 96,97, 98, 109, 112, 123, 125-127, 133, 147, 167

F
Filters   77
Five key messages   xviii-xix, 6, 117

G
Gathering   2, 58, 68, 73, 129, 135, 139, 143, 147, 151
Gathering Sheets   57-58, 69, 84, 131-132, 136, 140, 145, 149, 153
Goal Chart   118
Goals
   Attainable   117-118
   Measurable   115, 117-118
   Relevant   117-118
   Specific   102, 117
   Supported   117-118, 120-121
   Timing   100, 117-118
   Visible   117-118, 120

H
Having   xix, 23, 53, 56, 95-98, 106, 108, 109, 121
Hierarchy of needs   64
Honors   139-141

I
Interests   2, 5, 8, 28, 30-37, 38, 53-54, 55, 57, 58, 59, 64, 65, 69, 90, 111, 117, 124, 125, 130, 133, 135, 137, 141, 143, 146, 147

J
Job search   3, 9, 11, 116, 123, 135, 143
Joy   xv, 1, 2, 6, 7, 19, 23, 28, 30, 53, 64, 77, 84, 89, 95, 96, 100, 106, 108, 109, 111, 115, 117, 118, 124, 125, 137, 143, 156
Jung, Carl   xvii, 29, 44, 45, 162, 163

Index

L

Leadership   xvii, 59, 76, 81, 90-91, 94, 127, 135, 160, 161, 165, 167
Legacy Technique   44, 167
Letters of recommendation   143
Life Facets   2, 6, 20-22, 23, 101-106, 125, 133, 143, 146
   Citizenship   21, 105
   Economic   21, 105
   Health and fitness   21, 104
   Personal growth   21, 104
   Personal relations   21, 101, 104
   Play   21, 105
   Spiritual   21, 104
   Work/Career   21, 101, 102, 104
Life Interests   2, 28, 30-37, 38
   Application of technology   33
   Creative production   33
   Enterprise control   33
   Influence through language and ideas   33
   Managing people and relationships   33
   Quantitative analysis   33
   Teaching, counseling and mentoring   33
   Theory development and conceptual thinking   33
Life Purpose   xv, 2, 6, 9, 23-25, 29, 53, 55, 58, 67, 95, 97, 108-110, 113, 118, 123
Life Purpose Statement   2, 6, 23, 29, 53, 55, 67, 97, 98, 108-110

M

Maslow, Abraham   38, 46, 162
Motivators   29, 44, 46-52, 106, 124, 146
   Esteem   21, 46, 50-51, 64, 124
   Love   24, 38, 45, 46, 50-51, 57, 75, 78, 97, 111, 124, 151, 163
   Manifested actualization   46, 50-51, 124
   Physiological   38, 46, 50-51, 64, 124
   Power and control   46, 50-51
   Safety   38, 46, 50-51, 64, 81, 124
   Self-actualization   46, 50-51
   Transcendence   46, 50-51, 124

N

Needs as motivators   46, 51, 124

O

Objectives   84, 86, 87, 89

P

Passion   xv, 1, 2, 6, 23, 30, 53, 54, 58, 64, 66, 78, 96, 108, 117, 121, 123-127, 137, 156, 160
Personal Style   2, 8, 29, 44-55, 65, 112, 124, 135, 147, 151
Portfolio   1, 2, 3, 5, 12, 69, 100, 123, 129, 135, 140, 155-158
Power   xv, 1, 5, 7, 10, 21, 28, 30, 34, 44, 46, 50, 51, 53, 54, 61, 64, 66, 78, 96, 108, 117, 118, 121, 124, 125, 135, 137, 156, 160, 162
Preferences   29, 53, 64, 75, 95, 97, 98
Preferred Employer   2, 76, 84-89, 95-96, 97, 98, 125
   Expectations   84-85, 86-87, 89, 100, 125
   Objectives   84, 86, 87-88, 89
   Rewards and Recognition   84, 85-86, 87, 89
   Value System   84, 85, 87, 89
Professional memberships   147-150
Putting it all together   29, 53, 56, 58, 64, 68, 76, 95, 97, 98

R

References   10, 143, 151, 152-154
Resumé   2, 3, 11, 123, 124, 128, 151
Roles and Goals   2, 100, 101-107, 124, 143

S

Self-development   6, 130, 132, 133
Self-employment   69, 71
Significant emotional event   3
Skills   1, 2, 6, 8, 11, 30, 57-69, 72, 95, 99, 111, 112, 117, 124, 125, 126, 131, 132, 135, 136, 137, 143, 146, 147, 151
Story   5, 9, 11, 14, 15, 21, 34-36, 39-41, 47-49, 53, 60, 79-80, 99, 100, 154
Style   2, 6, 8, 28, 29, 44, 46, 47, 50-52, 53, 54, 55, 57, 64, 65, 76, 84, 90-93, 112, 124, 126, 127, 135, 147, 151

Success 5, 7, 9, 14, 30, 43, 45, 46, 57, 59, 61, 63, 67, 69, 71, 73, 84, 91, 97, 99, 119, 121, 124, 125, 127, 151, 159, 160, 167
Supervisors 75, 76

T
Talents 1, 8, 23, 57, 58, 59, 61, 63, 64, 67, 68, 69, 71, 73, 95, 123-125, 137, 139, 146, 167
Training 10, 11, 81, 125, 129-131, 167
Traits 2, 6, 28, 29, 38-43, 44, 45, 53, 54, 55, 64, 65, 112, 124, 125, 135, 146, 147, 151
True Values 2, 76, 77-83, 85, 95-96, 97, 98, 112, 124, 143, 146, 151

U
Using your portfolio 155, 158

V
Values
    External 2, 76, 77, 81-82
    Internal 76, 77-80, 81, 82, 124
Vocation 57, 64

W
Walkabout 27, 53, 162
Warren, Rick 23
Work and career goal chart 118
Work Environment 2, 9, 75-77, 81, 90-94, 95-96, 97,98, 112, 125, 133, 147
    Leadership 76, 90, 91, 94
    People 76, 90, 92
    Physical environment 76, 91, 93
    Work Style 8, 76, 90, 91-92, 127

Work examples 135-137, 148
Work Health Assessment 1, 6, 7-13, 123, 128, 160
    Automated 1, 7
    Personalized 7
Work in the home 69, 72
Work pyramid 64
Work Template 2, 116, 123-128, 133
    Job Search 123
    My Environment 125, 127
    My Needs 124, 126
    My Passion 124, 125
    My Talents 124, 125
    My Values 124, 126
    Rating 125-127
www.beingatwork.com 1, 7, 160, 167
www.beingatwork.blogs.com 160, 167
www.BobHunsberger.com 160, 167, 168
www.MaryBrandon.com 1, 7, 160, 161, 167, 168
www.PowerPassionJoy.com 161, 168
www.PrudenceCole.com 160, 161, 167, 168

Y
Your Stories 1, 6, 14-19, 29, 30, 34-37, 38, 39-41, 43, 44, 47-49, 50, 58, 60-63, 69, 77, 79-80, 81, 82, 124, 164

About the Authors

Mary Brandon, a gifted employment and motivation consultant and coach, established Aspect Consulting Inc. in 1991 with a basic mission of improving attitudes toward employment. However, personal and professional development has resulted in her broadening her focus to life perspectives. Aspect Consulting offers "The Legacy Technique (©2001-2006 by Aspect Consulting)" service and product line – which is at the heart of the philosophy that supports the activities within this book. Mary guides both individuals and organizations in identifying the incongruous thinking that is disabling them, integrating that knowledge to mobilize motivation and unveil gifts, talents, and purpose in the process.

This book reflects her belief that people – our most valuable resource – are their own expert, knowing best who they really are. Her clients have included state departments, non-profit human service organizations, corporations, small businesses, entrepreneurs, and individuals looking for a clearer perspective on their life and work.

Mary lives in the metropolitan Detroit area with her son, Traverse, and their pets.

Please visit: www.MaryBrandon.com

Prudence Cole is an accomplished leadership, work life and career coach who is committed to helping people find joy in work. Her background includes a highly successful career as a corporate executive. Long recognized for her leadership skills and talents, she continues to use her knowledge and gifts to support individuals in achieving leadership excellence.

Her company, being@work, Inc. is committed to working with businesses that recognize successful organizations *need productive, engaged employees*, and with individuals who desire work life success. Through her coaching, she has helped people transform their lives, resolve blockages and gaps and take responsibility for their happiness. This workbook originated out of her coaching practice and the needs of her clients.

Prudence lives in the metropolitan Detroit area with her husband, Richard Klimisch.

Please visit: www.PrudenceCole.com, www.beingatwork.com or beingatwork.blogs.com

Bob Hunsberger has over 40 years of experience in leadership and professional development training, in both military and corporate environments. His experience includes 28 years in the United States Marine Corps where he served in a variety of leadership positions – in combat, administration, and training. Upon completing a successful military career in 1977, Bob began his next career in a Fortune 500 corporation. Using his military training and experience, he was able to mentor and teach many individuals professional and leadership skills.

Retiring after 19 years, Bob started his own business, Robert S. Hunsberger Consulting, Inc., specializing in professional and personal development programs. He has provided services in employee training and development for clients throughout Michigan.

Bob lives in Bloomfield Hills, Michigan with his wife, Norma.

Please visit: www.BobHunsberger.com

To learn more about products and services to assist individuals, coaches and corporations, please visit:

www.powerpassionjoy.com

www.MaryBrandon.com

www.PrudenceCole.com

www.BobHunsberger.com

The authors' works are available on www.ReadingUp.com

Published by:
BookMarketingSolutions, LLC
The Publisher of Experts

The publisher of experts
www.BookMarketingSolutions.com